SELENA GO[...]

A Journey of Talent and Resilience

Note:

....

....

....

....

Douglas Glenn Rohde

CONTENTS

CHAPTER 1 - CHANGING THE GAME

CHAPTER 2 - GRAND PRAIRIE

CHAPTER 3 - LARGE BREAK

CHAPTER 4 - BARNEY

CHAPTER 5 - DISNEY CHANNEL

CHAPTER 6 - WIZARDS IN NEW YORK

CHAPTER 7 - TAYLOR

CHAPTER 8 - THE SCENE

CHAPTER 9 - RED CARPET

CHAPTER 10 - GOODWILL IN GHANA

CHAPTER 11 - FROM HOLLYWOOD TO HUNGARY

CHAPTER 12 - LOVE YOU LIKE A LOVE SONG

CHAPTER 13 - JELENA

CHAPTER 14 - DREAM DATE

CHAPTER 15 - WORLD TOUR

CHAPTER 16 - TIME OUT

CHAPTER 17 - THE HEART WANTS WHAT IT WANTS

CHAPTER 18 - TAKING CONTROL

CHAPTER 19 - MEXICO

CHAPTER 20 - REVIVAL

CHAPTER 21 - A FOREVER FRIEND

CHAPTER 22 - A21

CHAPTER 23 - HAPPY BIRTHDAY, SELENA

CHAPTER 1

THE GAME IS CHANGING

"I'm telling you to always trust yourself."

Selena Gomez crossed the stage to shake the hands of her front-row fans. Hundreds of hands reached up to grab hers as she did so. A piece of paper, her speech, was tucked beneath her right arm. But she never used it. She didn't have to. Selena knew exactly what she wanted to communicate to her WE Day audience in California. She told them she had always wanted to be an actor, but that when she was eleven, a casting director informed her she wasn't good enough.

"I'm sure you've all been told you're not good enough. It suffocates you. And it nearly did for me..."

It didn't seem conceivable. Is Selena Gomez, the singing sensation and actor with over 100 million social media followers, not enough? Everyone must have told her how amazing she was?

"But there was my mom, next to me," Selena explained, "and she said the most important thing was to always trust in myself." She encouraged me to keep going. I wouldn't be here if I didn't believe I could do it."

The audience fell silent as the charismatic young woman onstage told them about her mother, who had believed in her and worked four jobs to ensure Selena's success. Hearing Selena's tale and knowing she had endured was inspiring.

"I live a very blessed life," Selena explained to her admirers. "I have so much to be thankful for, and you play such an important role in inspiring me." You motivate me to do better. We should all strive to be better than we are."

The WE Day audience roared in applause. This is why they came: thousands of teenagers wanted to make the world a better place. WE Day was a global movement focused on taking action. It wasn't just adults who could make a difference in the world! The kids in the crowd had fantastic suggestions for improving their villages, cities, and even the planet. Seeing Selena onstage and hearing her passionate message gave them the confidence to trust in themselves and their abilities. Selena went on to discuss the pressures of celebrity, such as being told to look a certain way and act a certain way... "I'm sure you can all relate to this. You all deal with stress on a daily basis." Selena took a breather. Her expression was solemn.

"Up until lately, I had succumbed to that pressure. I had forgotten who I was. I tried to change who I am in the hopes that others would accept me for who I am."

Her voice had now cracked. Selena was on the edge of tears as she looked out at the sea of faces in front of her.

"And I realised I don't know how to be anything other than myself..."

Fans were hugging, crying, and grasping the hands of their friends next to them. Be true to yourself. Don't allow anyone to change your mind. It was the message they were looking for. Their protagonist spoke to them as if they were friends, sharing her worries and anxieties.

"Please just be kind to each other," Selena added. "Remain true to yourself. Please stay true to yourself and know that we have each other's backs. I've learned from my errors. I want you to know that I understand how you feel. You are the people you associate with. I hope I may encourage you to believe in yourself and your ability to love and be loved.

"Let's change the game," Selena said. "This is such a lovely thing you're doing. "You should be proud of yourself."

CHAPTER 2

GRAND PRAIRIE

Mandy Cornett was only fifteen years old when she discovered she was pregnant. Teen pregnancy was not uncommon in Grand Prairie, but Mandy was shocked. She was driven. When she graduated from high school, she aspired to be an actor. Having a child in her twenties? This was hardly the life she had envisioned for herself.

Mandy put on a brave mask, but she genuinely hoped she could flee. She was never popular in school. The other kids teased her because of her purple hair and combat boots. She didn't share their tastes in music, movies, or fashion. Mandy had always been unique. And now there was still a more compelling motive to target her...

Of course, everyone knew who Mandy's father was right away: Ricardo Gomez, or "Ricky" as everyone called him. Ricky was sixteen years old, one year older than Mandy. Will they remain together? Will they tie the knot? Everyone in the room had questions for the pair. It seemed like a soap opera, but it wasn't one Mandy and Ricky wanted to be a part of. So they sought counsel from their parents. Mandy and Ricky's parents were both happily married. They delivered the only response they had. Mandy and Ricky had no choice but to follow their hearts. The youngsters eventually made a decision: they would marry. They planned to return to high school when their kid was born to obtain the certifications they needed to find work. They knew it would be difficult, but they loved one other. Mandy and Ricky waited, nervous, scared, and happy, as the months passed and their new life came closer and closer.

Finally, Selena Marie Gomez was born on July 22, 1992. Selena, the baby, was the most beautiful thing her parents had ever seen. Her father's family was Mexican, and she got her father's dark hair and lengthy lashes. She inherited her mother's dark brown eyes. Mandy's heart felt like it was going to burst when she picked up her tiny child. She couldn't decide whether to laugh or cry as she lay in a hospital bed with her own parents beside her; she felt like a child and an adult at the same time. But every time she held her newborn baby in her arms, a flood of love washed away all her confusion.

Many couples dispute over baby names, but Mandy and Ricky agreed quickly... twice. Priscilla was their first option, but Selena's cousin Priscilla had only been born six months before. Instead, they named their infant Selena Quintanilla, a favourite artist who was also born in Texas. Mandy was sixteen at the time of Selena's birth, and Ricky was seventeen. Ricky's parents, Ricardo and Mary, and Mandy's parents, Debbie and David, agreed to look after the baby while the adolescents returned to school. So, from 8:30 a.m. until 4:00 p.m., the new parents pretended to be regular adolescent teens again. But the responsibility of having a baby had altered them, especially Mandy. She'd never worked hard in school. She had failed to comprehend the value of learning. But now she's started working... hard. Mandy wants to establish a good life for herself and her daughter Selena. Mandy rose from the bottom of the class to the top in the months that followed. She was first in her class by the time final examinations rolled around. She was also chosen as prom queen.

The girl with the purple hair suddenly seemed to have things sorted. Everything had changed for Mandy. Finally, now that school is over, Mandy and Ricky could be a family at last. Baby Selena was the apple of her parents' eye. Selena's grandparents adored her too, and they continued to help with childcare so that Mandy and Ricky could work. Cherished by all, Selena was growing fast: from a happy, healthy baby to a bouncing, energetic toddler, then a confident preschooler. Young Selena knew just how to get what she wanted – she might be small, but she was bold and full of character! And the way she imitated grownup behaviour made her parents howl with laughter. What would their little Selena be like as a teenager? At three and a half, she was already acting the part!

But life for Selena's parents was hard. As high-school graduates with little experience, they could expect only low wages for long hours. Every penny they earned was spent on food, rent, and fuel to run their car. There were no luxuries in the Gomez household – and with the pressure of having to support a family, Mandy's dream of being an actress seemed to be slipping away. She found herself waiting on tables and sweeping floors instead.

Selena's parents tried not to argue during the tough times, but it was difficult. There always seemed to be problems. Their fridge was broken. The car wouldn't start. There was a leak in the roof...

Mandy and Ricky started to blame each other for every small thing that went wrong. The one ray of sunshine? Bright, bubbly, playful Selena. She kept them smiling, no matter what. Her laughter and her big, beautiful grin were infectious. But by the time Selena turned five, Ricky and Mandy had become so unhappy in their marriage that they began to question whether they should stay together. They were worried the tension in the house wasn't good for Selena either.

"We can't go on like this," Mandy told Ricky. "It's not working."

Ricky nodded. "We need to get a divorce."

It was the first time in months that the couple had agreed on anything.

"We've done the best we could," Mandy sighed. They looked at each other – both were thinking the same thing. Telling their daughter would be the hardest thing in the world.

They were right. Five-year-old Selena's eyes were wide with horror as her parents explained that they had decided to split up.

"But you can't! We're a family," she cried.

"We'll be happier if we live apart, mija," explained Ricky.

"What about me? I want to live with both of you!"

"We love you very much," Mandy told her. "Nothing will change that – ever. You'll just have two homes instead of one."

But little Selena knew that everything would change. On the TV programmes she watched, when parents divorced, mums got new boyfriends and dads got new girlfriends. And the new partners were always horrible to their new stepchildren. Always.

"I hate you! Both of you!" Selena stomped out of the room, slamming the door behind her.

"Selena! Come back!"

But Selena refused.

Over the next few weeks, she wouldn't listen to anything her parents said to reassure her. The only people she could talk to were her grandparents.

"You're scared right now, but it's going to be OK, honey," Nana Debbie told her. "Your mom and your dad will always be there for you – and so will we."

"We sure will." Grandpa David smiled.

Debbie and David felt like second parents to Selena. She had spent so much time with them when she was little. If they said it was going to be OK, maybe it would. But she couldn't get rid of the nugget of worry in her chest – and she couldn't help blaming her parents for breaking up their family. It would take a long time to change that. Time passed, and like Nana had said, the important things did stay the same. Selena still spent time with both her parents. She lived with Mandy, and Ricky came to take her out at weekends. Slowly, as she got used to it, not being together as a family felt a little less painful.

However, money was still an issue. Mandy wanted Selena to have everything other girls had as she grew older: clothes, trips to amusement parks and museums, CDs, concerts... She could tell her daughter was passionate about music. Mandy had to work four jobs at times simply to make ends meet. On the way to school, the automobile would occasionally run out of gas. There was little money for vacations or other luxuries, and Mandy despised asking Debbie and David for assistance. Selena's mother was still looking for work as an actress in addition to her other professions. She was adamant about not giving up on her dream. Grand Prairie was too tiny to provide many possibilities, so when the perfect roles arose, Mandy travelled across Texas with Selena. Taking Selena to the theatre was less expensive than hiring a babysitter! Despite the fact that Mandy had brought books and toys for Selena to play with, her daughter's focus was constantly on the stage. Selena enjoyed seeing her mother act, and she had strong beliefs of her own...

"You know, Mom, it might be funnier if you did it differently," she said as she watched Mandy rehearsing a comedy.

Her mother laughed. Selena's favourite activity was putting on plays with her pals. She was always the director, ordering everyone where to stand and how to recite their lines. "How do you think I should go about it then?" she inquired of her daughter. Selena's expression was solemn. "It would be better if you paused longer before saying your final word." You may also place your hands on your hips or anything. Perhaps you could roll your eyes? That would be amusing."

Those proposals weren't half bad. Mandy's six-year-old kid had a great sense of what would and wouldn't work onstage! And Selena's talent wasn't limited to directing others. She could play any role: witches, princesses, pirates, and so on. Her favourite roles were comedic ones, and she could impersonate anyone. Selena's impersonations of Mandy's co-stars were amusing - and sometimes painfully true!

"She's going to be an actress, I'm certain of it," Mandy assured Debbie. "She's far more confident than I was at her age."

"She's got a special talent," Selena's grandmother concurred. "Take a look at the shows she puts on. All those different voices, all those different parts... She's incredible."

It was correct. Selena sparkled in all she did: singing, dancing, and acting. But, Mandy pondered, will there be enough possibilities for a rising young actress in Grand Prairie?

CHAPTER 3

LARGE BREAK

"Pay attention, Selena. A casting call for Barney and Friends will be held! "See you next weekend!"

Mandy's face was flushed with delight. She had seen a casting announcement on the bulletin board at the theatre where she worked and had rushed home as quickly as she could to notify her daughter. One of the most popular children's shows on television was Barney. Why wasn't Selena more enthusiastic?

"Barney's only for babies, Mom!"

Selena was nine years old. She was in third grade at the time. She didn't watch Barney and Friends any longer!

"Sweetheart, the children on the show aren't babies." They're all of various ages."

Selena smirked. "Really?"

"Yes! I believe you should try out. You'd get to perform... and sing."

Mandy was well aware that this would pique Selena's interest. Her child enjoyed singing. Her voice was excellent - smooth and clear, mature for her age. Britney Spears was Selena's idol. She repeatedly performed Britney's songs and dance moves.

"You'll make new friends, too," Mandy remarked.

Selena put on a serious expression. Barney was clearly aimed at children... but it would be proper acting. "I want to do it," she finally said. Mandy hugged her. "That's fantastic, honey. Perhaps we might watch a few Barney episodes to prepare for the audition?"

"Sure." Selena made a funny face.

But Selena secretly adored the giant purple dinosaur and his pals. She remembered watching the show as a child at her grandparents' house.

"Can I have a cookie and some milk while we're watching?"

Her mother laughed. "Didn't someone just say they weren't a baby?!"

On a Saturday afternoon, an audition for Barney and Friends was held. Mandy had brought her daughter to countless TV and theatre auditions by this point, so Selena knew just what to do. First and foremost, she waited in line at the desk to jot down her name and address. There were already hundreds of names on the list!

Selena looked around the room uneasily. It was jam-packed with kids and their parents. Despite what her mother had said, she was the oldest.

"Those kids are still in diapers," she said quietly.

"They're not!" Mandy said. "They must number at least five."

Selena smirked. "How do they learn their lines if they're only five?" she enquired.

However, the girl behind them in line appeared to be her age. Selena looked up to her mother, who encouraged her. Selena grinned. "Hello, my name is Selena Gomez. "Can you tell me your name?"

"I'm Demi Lovato," the girl said, confidently smiling. "I'm originally from Dallas."

"I'm from Grand Prairie," Selena explained.

After a brief pause, the two females said simultaneously, "Who is your favourite singer?"

They both laughed. In an instant, Selena and Demi forgot about the audition and started dating. Britney Spears was a favourite of both girls. Demi was learning to play the piano. When she grew up, Selena aspired to be an actress and singer. Selena competed in beauty pageants on occasion. Their anniversaries were only one month apart. They have so many things in common!

"Do you want to colour?" Demi said after they'd told each other everything they could think of. She took a book from her backpack. "Here, we can sit on my coat."

However, then... The casting director's assistant exclaimed, "Selena Gomez!" "Please come through."

"It's time," her mother said.

"Good luck!" Demi exclaimed.

"You, too," Selena murmured, squeezing her new best friend's hand.

What a dream come true if she and Demi both earned roles on the program! Selena had almost forgotten about the casting after a month had passed. It was July 22nd, and she had more fascinating things to think about today. Her birthday has arrived! She was ten years old. Debbie and David, her grandparents, had planned a family gathering. Ricky and her cousin Priscilla would be there. Selena was giddy with delight. Coloured decorations were fluttering in the treetops, and a table was laid with all of Selena's favourite goodies. Everyone had brought a gift, and Selena had shrieked with excitement as she unwrapped them. She and her mother didn't have many luxuries, but she felt like a princess today. Best of all, her grandmother had cooked a massive cake with white and pink icing. Her family came to sing "Happy Birthday," but just as Selena was about to cut the cake, her mother intervened.

"I have one more present for you, Selena."

Mandy presented her with a large envelope. It was addressed to Selena Marie Gomez and appeared to be formal. Selena felt a tingle of nervousness run up her spine. Her entire family was staring at her. Did they have any idea what was inside? She ripped open the envelope, took out the wad of paper inside, and began reading: Dear Selena Gomez, We are thrilled to offer you the role of Gianna after your recent audition for a role on Barney and Friends... Selena put down her book and looked around at her family. Her eyes widened in amazement.

"I've got a role!" "Come on, Barney!"

Mandy, Ricky, and the rest of the family broke out laughing. Her cousin, Priscilla, who understood how badly Selena wanted to be an actress, was the most vocal.

"Wow," Selena exclaimed. That's incredible!"

Selena was taken aback. "How did you know?" she inquired of her mother. "How did you know it was a yes' and not a'no'?"

Mandy grinned. "The letter arrived this morning." Because the envelope was so thick, I knew you'd gotten a part. It indicated that there was a contract within!" Yes, there was. Selena was holding her very first contract in her hands. She'd made it as an actress! This had to be the nicest birthday present anyone has ever received! There was just one more thing that would make it absolutely perfect...

CHAPTER 4

BARNEY

"You've got a part, too!"

Selena and Demi leaped up and down, holding each other's hands. It was the first day of rehearsals, and their excitement was palpable. They were supposed to appear on the show together!

"What's the name of your character?" Selena inquired.

"Angela! "How about you?"

"Gianna! "It's Italian, according to Mom."

Selena and Demi became fast friends. When they weren't in front of the camera, they were telling stories and cracking jokes, listening to music and chatting about boys. The girls also spent a lot of time together in front of the camera. They joined Barney the Dinosaur to sing songs and perform games, demonstrating to young viewers how to utilise their imagination, collaborate, and express their emotions. There was a lot to learn. First, there were lines to memorise and actions to do correctly. Then they had to figure out where they should stand for each segment of the episode. "Blocking" was the term for this. With a large dinosaur and a swarm of children in each scene, it was often difficult to get it right.

The director screamed out, "Gianna!" "You're concealing Angela. Please move slightly to the left..."

"Masking" meant to stand in front of someone. It happened all the time in the first few weeks as they learned where the cameras were.

"Gianna!"

Demi stroked Selena's shoulder. "He's talking to you," she said quietly.

"Oh! Sorry!" On set, Selena hadn't gotten used to being addressed by her character name.

"Also, don't look directly at the camera." Just keep an eye out for it and keep your face visible."

It was difficult at first because there were so many things to consider. But the girls quickly learned where to look, when to move, and how to say their lines. Running around an artificial plastic garden with a massive purple dinosaur felt... perfectly natural! But there was an issue. Selena and Demi were tormented at school for performing in a children's show. A show for infants.

"I hate it," Demi said to Selena after a particularly difficult week. "I don't want to go to school anymore."

"Perhaps the bullies are just jealous," Selena speculated.

"I don't mind. Demi informed her, "I want to be homeschooled." "I've asked my mom."

The other kids might have been jealous, but that didn't stop the insults from hurting. Selena, like her companion, disliked going to school. It didn't seem fair that a pleasant purple dinosaur was complicating her life. Selena was also worried about something else. Ever since her parents divorced, she had been terrified of them finding new companions, whether it was a new boyfriend for Mandy or a new girlfriend for Ricky. Stepmothers and stepfathers were always evil in fiction and on television. Take a look at Cinderella! Selena understood she had to keep Mandy and Ricky from making wrong decisions. What if, like Cinderella's father, they were blinded by love? Selena kept a close eye on things. She even devised a battery of tests to see whether the new boyfriend or girlfriend was suitable. Mandy eventually met someone who passed both her own and Selena's tests! Brian Teefey was his name. He was entertaining and kind, and Selena could see how happy he made her mother. At first, accepting a new member of their family was difficult. But as the months passed, Selena discovered she was able to accept Brian into their lives. Ricky will always be her father, but Brian held a special place in her heart as well.

Selena spent two years on Barney. She'd made a lot of friends on the program, but they were all leaving one by one. It was now Selena and Demi's turn. They were getting too old to be in a preschool show at the age of twelve. Selena was sad to say goodbye to the friendly purple dinosaur, but she was far too old for clapping games and singing numbers songs!

"What am I supposed to do now, Mom?" When they arrived home after the last day of filming, Selena asked Mandy. She felt empty on the inside. She despised the idea of going to school every day. She knew she'd miss her Barney pals and her time at the studio.

Mandy embraced her. She despised seeing her daughter sad.

"We'll go to some auditions," she said to Selena. "You're 12. You have so many options now."

And it wasn't long until the ideal audition presented itself.

CHAPTER 5

DISNEY CHANNEL

"Let's go ahead and do the goat scene," Selena was advised by the casting director. "You can start whenever you're ready."

It might have sounded strange to anybody else, but Selena was more than prepared for "the goat scene." She had been practising it for weeks. Her character had assisted in the theft of a goat and now desired to restore it. Because Selena didn't have the rest of the screenplay, she had no idea why - or what would happen!

Selena clutched the script in her palm without looking at it. She knew every word by heart. Instead, she concentrated on her expression. A camera was in front of her; she was being filmed for the team of directors and producers to watch later.

"You stole the goat?" Selena's eyes widened in amazement.

The lines that were not Selena's were read aloud by the casting director. The action started right away. Selena managed to sound increasingly irritated with each word she spoke. She was determined to return the goat to its rightful place!

"Good," the casting director said. "Do it one more time."

The second time around went even better. Selena added extra levity to her phrases. Confusion. Exasperation. Despair is amusing.

"You did an excellent job," the casting director said. "So, Selena, what do you like to do in your spare time when you're not acting?"

That was simple. "I love hanging out with my friends," Selena explained. "And I'm going to the mall with my mom."

"Do you sing, too?"

Selena gave a nod. She stated that her ambition was to become a singer like her idol, Britney Spears, when she grew up. She preferred to act first and then sing later. She had everything planned out in her brain! "And do you have any favourite television shows?" the casting director inquired. Selena smiled. Lizzie McGuire, That's So Raven... were among her favourites. The casting director gave a friendly smile. "So, do you like the Disney Channel?" Selena gave a nod. It was true, thankfully. Because Selena's audition was for the Walt Disney Company!

"I was sitting out there listening to you and your friends," the casting director explained, motioning to a room outside where Demi and some of Selena's other Barney friends were waiting for their auditions. "You're so funny."

Selena smiled with delight. Anything involving her buddies made her happy!

The audition had concluded. Back in the waiting room, Mandy wrapped her arms around her daughter and squeezed her tightly. "How did it go, honey?"A

Selena grinned. "The casting director was quite pleasant. She inquired about my background in acting, as well as my singing abilities. "I believe it went well."

Mandy grinned. Her 12-year-old daughter never got carried away. Speaking to her was like speaking to an adult, especially when it came to acting. But Mandy understood that beneath her icy appearance, Selena desired nothing more than to be on the Disney Channel. It wasn't long before wonderful news arrived. Selena had landed her first film job! Spy Kids is an adventure comedy in which I play a little role. Everything was significantly bigger on Spy Kids than it was on Barney. There were more cameras, more personnel, and more actors. Selena was also filming for the first time on site. Each of the hair, make-up, and costuming departments had their own trailer. It was really unique and amazing! Selena longed for her next assignment as soon as the filming was completed. The months passed. Finally, she was offered a small part in Walker, Texas Ranger, which was also shot on location. Then Selena waited some more. New auditions were held and then cancelled. Silence. "Be patient," Mandy said. But all Selena wanted was to be back on set!

Selena finally got the call she'd been waiting for: the Disney Channel wanted her! They asked her to appear as a guest star on The Suite Life of Zack and Cody, an adolescent sitcom.

Wow! Everyone was talking about Suite Life. Forget Barney... Nobody would make fun of her for being on Suite Life! The producers had also recognized Selena's great singing voice and requested her to record one of the show's soundtrack tracks. Her first ever recording!

Another first...

Selena played Cody's girlfriend, Gwen, who is cast in a school production of A Midsummer Night's Dream alongside his best friend Zack. Gwen and Zack fall in love while acting out a scene, much to the dismay of Zack's girlfriend, Vanessa. The script was hilarious and full of twists and turns. Selena liked it, however...

"Eww! "Do Gwen and Zack have to kiss?"

Selena had never kissed anyone before, on or off set.

Demi was called.

"What if I can't do it?" she exclaimed.

"You're an actor," Demi said. "Of course you can."

"But it's not just a quick kiss," Selena bemoaned. "It's like a minute long!"

"You'll be fine," Demi chuckled. "It might even be enjoyable!"

Demi was partly correct. It wasn't entertaining, but it was adequate. It seemed strange to believe that thousands of viewers would watch her first on-screen kiss months later! A year later, in 2006, Selena, then fourteen, was cast in her biggest part yet: Mikayla Skeech, Hannah Montana's singing-star rival. Hannah Montana was the most popular show on the Disney Channel, so this was a significant step. Miley Cyrus, who played Hannah, was already a great star, and she and Selena became fast friends. Plus, it was exciting to portray a villain because Mikayla was so nasty!

Selena, on the other hand, appeared in only two episodes. She felt the same way after filming ended. Her dream part has yet to materialise.

One casting director was direct with her. "You just don't have what it takes for a lead role."

It was difficult to understand. But maybe it's true, thought Selena. She realised how fortunate she was to be doing something she enjoyed at the age of 14. But perhaps she wasn't cut out for a career as an actor. Maybe she just didn't have what Miley Cyrus had. Maybe she wasn't cut out to be a star. Mandy, on the other hand, was adamant. "All that matters is that you believe you can do it. Have faith in yourself. Let the critics be critics, and simply listen to yourself. "Don't give up, Selena."

Selena continued on with her mother's words in her heart.

CHAPTER 6

LAW IN NEW YORK

Alex Russo, a newcomer in Selena's life, was the name she had heard. Alex resided in New York with her family, who owned Waverly Place, a sandwich business. Her two brothers were older and younger. She was cool, humorous, confident, and occasionally caustic, and she always knew how to get what she wanted... especially from her father, Jerry. She adored her friends and would go to great lengths for her family.

There was also a twist: Alex's family were wizards.

Alex Russo played the title character in the new sitcom Wizards of Waverly Place. It was supposed to premiere on the Disney Channel in 2007. Selena liked the sound of it because she enjoyed family comedies. She filtered out the comments of the casting director who had told her she couldn't play a main role while waiting for her audition. She might be able to. She was well aware of it. Selena's Wizards audition was the finest she'd ever done. Something about the position appealed to me. Alex was right for Selena, and Selena was right for Alex.

Almost immediately, the casting director called. Selena had the part!

The most fantastic thing that had occurred to Selena was landing the role of Alex Russo. Finally, she was in command! Selena, on the other hand, was filled with trepidation as well as enthusiasm. She and Mandy would have to relocate to Los Angeles for filming. It would be vast, bustling, and fast-paced, unlike little Grand Prairie. Would she be accepted? Will she make new friends? Will her Grand Prairie friends still contact her from so far away?

But, as Mandy always said, faith in herself and everything would be well. Selena knew she'd love playing Alex Russo from the first day of rehearsals. She adored the character, and she had a great time hanging out with the other young actors. Selena's on-screen brothers, Justin and Max, were played by David Henrie and Jake T. Austin, respectively. It was exciting for me as an only child to suddenly have two siblings. Selena, David, and Jake spent so much time together that they soon felt like a family. Selena fell in love with the show's colourful, welcoming set as well. The "loft" where the Russos lived had the New York skyline painted on the windows. There was the sandwich store, where Alex and her brothers assisted their parents by waiting tables and doing the dishes. Then there were the Greenwich Village-style street scenes, complete with red-brick buildings, ivy trailing from window boxes, and vividly coloured street art... Finally, there was the wizard lair, a secret room filled with potions and magical instruments where Alex and her brothers learnt magic from their father - and which also served as their entrance to the wizard realm.

The world behind the scenes was just as enchanting. There was rail after rail of apparel for each of the characters in the wardrobe department - casual clothes, party ensembles, fancy dress... Alex has a lot more clothes than Selena! The hair and make-up stations were also fascinating. The crew spent hours meticulously changing actors into various creatures such as werewolves, ghouls, and monsters. Not all of the activity could be captured on the set. Selena and the other cast members acted in front of the "green screen" at times. The images would then be placed on other background visuals, such as the New York skyline. Selena's character had to learn to pilot a flying carpet over the city's rooftops in the first episode. At least, that's how it seemed on television! Selena was actually positioned uncomfortably on a mat thrown over some enormous boxes. The shaky contraption felt as shaky as a flying carpet! Selena and her on-screen father, David DeLuise, fell off it repeatedly as they attempted to steer around corners and avoid skyscrapers.

"Call it father-daughter bonding," DeLuise chuckled as they collided again on the floor. Maria Canals-Barrera, a Latina actress, played Selena's on-screen mother, Theresa, a mortal. Selena had never given any regard to her South American ancestors. Her father's mother and father were both Mexican, although her family was not very traditional. Then one day, in the street, a mother went up to her, waving to get her attention.

"My kids love you," she said to Selena. "We're Mexican, and seeing someone who looks like them on TV is very important to them." Thank you very much!"

"But I haven't done anything," Selena exclaimed, astonished. "I'm just a kid on a kids' show."

"You're an inspiration!" Latino children can believe in their dreams because they see you."

Selena was filled with pride. She enjoyed the concept of influencing young children. Her own childhood had been difficult, and she knew how difficult it was to keep believing in oneself. If she could help others, that was more powerful than any spell Alex could conjure with her wizard's wand!

The plot of Wizards follows the three Russo children, Alex, Justin, and Max, as they compete to become the Family Wizard, following in the footsteps of their father, Jerry. Only one individual in a magical family has the ability to keep the family's powers.

The characters were well-liked by the public, and the show swiftly gained popularity. New actors soon joined the cast. Alex's best friend, Harper Finkle, was played by Jennifer Stone, and Alex finally gained a lover, Mason Greenback, who was charming, talented, British... and a werewolf.

Alex quickly discovered that dating a werewolf was not simple. Mason tried his hardest to repress his werewolf nature, but there was only one thing that might keep the couple together indefinitely: Alex had to win the challenge to become the Family Wizard, which would make her immortal. The fans hoped and waited!

The stakes were high on-screen, and they were even higher off-screen. Selena's celebrity grew in tandem with the growth of Wizards. It felt incredible to hear that so many people enjoyed her program and wanted to learn more about her. However, it could become overwhelming at times. Social media was expanding, and it was so simple to spread rumours, real or false. Selena tried to be herself, but it was impossible for her to relax. She was concerned about what the media would say, as well as what her followers would think. Do they like her new hairstyle? Could she eat out without getting photographed? Could she put her trust in new people she met? Nothing in her life, big or small, was any longer private - and it sucked.

Selena was surrounded by a group of hardworking people who were all dedicated to making her career a success. Her publicist, personal assistant, and managers included her mother, Mandy, and stepfather, Brian. Mandy couldn't express how proud she was of her 16-year-old daughter. Every day, she was astounded by what talented, kind-hearted Selena had accomplished. And the most amazing thing? Selena had only recently begun. Mandy was aware of how much more she had to offer.

Managing Selena's hectic TV career left Mandy with little time to unwind. However, a valuable hour had been freed up between meetings this afternoon. Mandy made a beeline for one of her favourite spots, the Barnes & Noble bookstore, while Selena was at the studio rehearsing. She enjoyed reading, and the tables stacked high with best-sellers were enticing. She began to look around. Unlike the steamy, crowded streets of Los Angeles, the atmosphere inside the store was serene.

Mandy strolled into the historical fiction department, then the romance section, and finally the fantasy section. Her attention was drawn to a display of thrillers, specifically a beautiful cover depicting a girl sitting on a swing. She chose a duplicate. 13 Arguments. It was a book for teenagers.

A shudder ran down Mandy's spine as she read the blurb. She paid for her book and began reading it in the cab on her way to her next appointment.

Mandy couldn't put the book down once she got started. And then she had an idea...

"Honey, I want you to read this," she told Selena as she handed her the book. "I think we should meet with the writer."

"Why, Mom?" Selena inquired.

"You'll grow out of Disney one day." I want you to have some incredible projects ready for when that time arrives."

"And do you think this book would make good TV?"

"TV or a film," Mandy suggested. "You'd be fantastic in the lead. We might have creative control if we purchased the rights. "Our very own show!"

Selena adored the concept, as well as the novel. Life after Disney seemed so far away, but Mandy was correct: she would be too old for the Wizarding World one day.

"Let's go meet the author," she said.

Who knew what the future held? Selena, on the other hand, couldn't wait for projects as fascinating as this one.Meanwhile, Selena Gomez, the Disney star, was busier than ever. Mandy had set up ads, interviews, and even her debut music video in the weeks between filming Wizards. 'Burnin' Up' by the Jonas Brothers - Joe, Nick, and Kevin - was the song. What is Selena's role? Nick's beautiful love interest. Although it was a minor role, the filming would transform her life. Nick Jonas had recently broken up with Hannah Montana star Miley Cyrus. Selena, who was humorous, confident, and talented, blew him away. Selena had the same reaction. She'd never had a meaningful relationship before. Nick was her first celebrity boyfriend, a rising talent who became a household name after performing the highly popular 'Introducing Me'.

But it wasn't Nick who made a difference in Selena's life.Taylor Swift was the one. Taylor also appeared on the set as Joe's love interest. The two girls hit it off right away. Both were friendly, open, and generous. They had a similar sense of comedy. Taylor knew the pressures of celebrity, but she also saw the lighter side of life in the spotlight. Selena believed she could tell Taylor whatever she wanted. She was confident that her secrets would be kept safe.

Taylor was also dating Nick's brother, Joe. Selena exclaimed, "Double dates!" "Can we?"

But when Nick insisted on strolling 10 metres ahead of her on a double date in New York's Central Park, Selena began to have second thoughts about her new partner. She enjoyed being candid and honest with her admirers. She and Nick were in a relationship. What if the general public saw them together? Taylor stayed behind to walk with her pal.

"What's wrong with Nick?" Selena asked quietly. "Is he embarrassed for us to be seen together?"

Taylor pressed her hand across her friend's arm. "If he can't handle it, that's his problem."

"We're all together." Why can't we just be honest like regular people?" Selena smirked. There was nothing wrong with being concerned for someone. It didn't feel right to keep it hidden.

"Boys are dumb," Taylor remarked. "It's friendship that really counts."

It was correct. Nick and Selena's relationship ended quickly, as did Taylor and Joe's. Selena, on the other hand, had discovered someone who actually understood her in Taylor Swift. She was certain they would be lifelong friends.

Fortunately, Selena didn't have much time to worry about boys. Her profile was steadily rising, and she now had an intriguing new addition to her resume: animated films. Selena's warm, deep voice and impeccable comic timing put her in high demand.

She first voiced Princess Selenia in Arthur and the Revenge of Maltazard, then Mavis in Hotel Transylvania (one of Selena's favourite productions!). In the film Horton Hears a Who! Selena played all 96 of Mayor Whoville's daughters. Voice acting was an odd experience, very different from being on a TV set. Each of the stars recorded their parts independently. Selena never met her on-screen father, the Mayor, or Jim Carrey, who portrayed Horton. Perhaps one day! It wasn't simply Selena's acting career that was flourishing. Selena had always had a passion for singing. She'd known since she was seven years old that she wanted to be a singer, and now Disney had given her an incredible opportunity. They were interested in signing her to their Hollywood Records label. Selena's sixteenth birthday coincided with the delivery of the news. It had all come true! But she had one requirement: she wanted to sing in a band. She didn't want to be a solo performer. At least not yet. Disney concurred. Selena's musical adventure has begun.

CHAPTER 8

THE SCENE

Every band requires excellent musicians, which Selena and her team set out to recruit. Selena desired to be present at all stages. She desired for her band to be the greatest it could be!

They finally chose four excellent players after weeks of auditions: Ethan on lead guitar and backup vocals, Joey on bass guitar, Greg on drums, and Nick on keyboard. They also settled on a band name: Selena Gomez and the Scene.

Selena enjoyed spending time with the boys since their musical knowledge was astounding. Cadence? Bridge? Key to the house? Riff? Is that an instrumental tag? Elision? Selena couldn't keep up when the males started talking about music and songwriting!

"How do you know all this stuff?!" In astonishment, Selena inquired. She had collaborated with a producer to record the Wizards theme song, but Ethan and the others were more technical.

"I've been playing since I could hold a guitar," Ethan replied, and the others agreed.

"Same," they said.

"It's like you and acting," Joey continued. "You're doing it all the time, so the technical stuff is second nature."

Selena was well aware that she had a lot to learn, but she was fortunate to have excellent tutors. Ethan and the other members of the band trained her to play the guitar and the drums. She was also taking singing classes to help her voice.

"I make mistakes. A lot. "No one is perfect," Selena said on her vlog. But she enjoys being pushed beyond her comfort zone; it was enjoyable to be learning new things. Practice would eventually lead to perfection. Selena was also working with some of the top music producers in America, including Ted Bruner, Tim James, and Antonina Armato - a production partnership known as Rock Mafia - and drummer Gina Schock. It was critical to find the perfect sound for the band's debut record.

"Whose music do you like?" Ted inquired.

Selena made no hesitations. She mentioned her favourite bands. "Paramore. Forever the Sickest Children. Britney."

"And what do you want to say?" Gina inquired.

That was more difficult. Selena reflected on her favourite songs. What were their key themes? Love, celebrity, being oneself... She wished to write a song about her experience. She wanted to demonstrate to her fans who she was.

Selena and her producers listened to hundreds of tracks together. These were sent to them from songwriters from all over the world, all of whom were eager to have Selena and her band play their work. There were decent tunes, fantastic songs, and even some bad songs!

"Listen to this," Selena said, laughing. "It's about time for a swimming lesson!"

"And this guy has rhymed the words 'laugh' and' sloth'!" Gina elaborated. "Seriously?!"

"A sloth-themed song?" That one has to be used!" Selena laughed. Some of these tunes were so amusing that she couldn't envision anyone ever recording them. But, song after song, the album began to take shape.

Her producers wrote many of the best tunes. Ted, Tim, Antonina, and Gina were all accomplished songwriters. 'I Won't Apologise,' however, was Selena's personal favourite. What was her message? Never alter your personality to please others. Selena Gomez and The Scene were finally ready for their first studio session after months of practice and hours spent writing and rearranging songs. Selena couldn't contain her enthusiasm as she arrived at the studio with the band. Making an album! For the first time ever! She realised how fortunate she was as she glanced about at the people who had made it happen - her band, her incredible producers, and her bright mother Mandy. Her name would be in bold letters on the record cover, but this was a massive collaborative effort.

Selena and Ted had chosen a song named 'Falling Down' written by Gina, Ted, and another producer, Trey Vittetoe, as the lead single. The theme was Hollywood living. Selena appreciated how the song mocked celebrities. She despised how superficial and phoney Hollywood life could be at times.

"Let's record 'Falling Down' first," Ted suggested. "Selena, are you ready?"

He didn't need to inquire. Selena was in the vocal booth, headphones on, before he had finished speaking. "Let's go!" says one. Ted signalled her. Selena began to sing as the red recording light flashed. The singing lessons had paid off. Selena's voice had always been powerful, but her tone was improving. It was rich, warm, and expressive.

"That was fantastic, Selena. "Wonderful," Ted replied after she was through. "Can you try it again with more bite?"

"Bite? "You mean, sound angry?" Selena inquired.

"Well, sort of. Mocking, I suppose. You're making fun of the concept of celebrity."

"OK, you got it." Selena was a famous actress. She excelled at instilling the appropriate emotion. She concentrated on her persona and sung the song again, her teeth biting into the lyrics. Ted was correct: bite was precisely what the music required!

Through the glass panel that separated the voice booth from the console where Ted was manipulating the sound, Ted gave her a thumbs up. "Perfect! "I've had an idea..."

Ted repeated Selena's statements to her. They sounded exactly like she had recorded them. Selena couldn't help but cringe when she realised she was recording her own voice without a backup track. Especially in a crowded place!

"Now see what you think of this," Ted suggested.

He listened to the recording again. This time, though, everything was different. It was still her voice, but... Selena said, "It's way more sassy!" "Wow! "How did you accomplish that?" Ted had altered Selena's voice with a synthesiser to make it seem more electronic. The sound was excellent for the song's lyrics. Following that, Ethan, Joey, Greg, and Nick recorded their bits.

"Really go for it, guys," Ted encouraged. "Especially drums and guitars." Make them as aggressive as possible."

Greg and Ethan channelled their inner rock stars on drums and lead guitar. Selena whooped on the opposite side of the glass. "Wow, that was incredible. You guys are awesome!" There were 12 more songs to record over the next four months, and the recording studio came to seem like a second home to Selena, Ethan, and the rest of the band. Selena's technical abilities and understanding of the recording process improved with each session. She couldn't believe how much she'd discovered. Selena chose the title Kiss & Tell with the help of her producers and the record label. What is the next step? Creating a cover image. Selena had an idea: a basic close-up of a face with a jewelled heart on top of the lips. The gems represented fame, which was a significant motif throughout the record. When the art director answered yes, Selena was overjoyed! Of course, the face would be Selena's. She was used to seeing herself on posters, televisions, and magazine covers by this point, but seeing her face on the front of her debut album cover was a dream come true!

CHAPTER 9

RED CARPET

Kiss & Tell was published on September 29, 2009, and that same night, Selena and her band performed on Dancing with the Stars for the first time. The show drew millions of viewers from throughout the country. The stakes were high!

They chose 'Falling Down' to sing. While Ethan and the boys dressed down in jeans and T-shirts, Selena dressed up in a gold sequin playsuit and long, sparkly earrings. It was difficult not to be distracted by the professional dancers, Derek and Karina, who performed a spectacular routine on the dance floor in front of Selena, but she remained focused. She strolled boldly across the floor, her gaze fixed on the camera whenever it panned in on her face. Her acting abilities were coming in handy. As Selena reached the end of the song and Derek and Katrina took their last postures, there was thunderous clapping. She applauded the dancers, and they applauded back. Another fantastic team effort!

Selena and the boys worked tirelessly in the months that followed, taking advantage of every opportunity to promote the record on TV, radio, and online. They sang Tim and Antonina's song 'Naturally' on The Ellen DeGeneres Show in December. They played with Justin Bieber at PopCon just two months later, in February. Selena Gomez and the Scene also started on their first tour, which included 18 gigs in the United States and one in London.

And the end consequence of their efforts? Kiss & Tell peaked at number nine in the United States. Selena was overjoyed. Her debut record was a smash! It didn't seem real. Selena felt as if she was living two lives. She was spending more and more time in the recording studio and performing with The Scene as a singer. When she wasn't singing, she was back on the set of Wizards, holding a magic wand. She was also starring in her first film, Another Cinderella Story. Singer? Actress? TV? Film? Selena had trouble remembering who she was meant to be from one day to the next!

The Wizards cast received some wonderful news in September of 2009. The first season of the show was nominated for Outstanding Children's Program at the 61st Emmy Awards, America's most prestigious television honour. Are you up against them? Hannah Montana and iCarly are two examples. Selena was a fan of both shows. She had known Miley Cyrus since she appeared on Hannah Montana the previous year. Could they truly win against this level of competition?

The event was scheduled to take place at the Nokia Theater in Los Angeles, one of the largest theatres in the United States. Selena had walked the red carpet at a few film premieres and music awards previously, but nothing had prepared her for this. The entire Hollywood A-list would be there, posing for photos one after the other, the women in long, gilded gowns and the guys in tuxedos.

"What am I going to wear?" Selena inquired of Mandy. "I'll need a ballgown, won't I?"

Selena examined hundreds of dresses in a variety of colours and styles. Should she go for something traditional? Satin? Silk? Maybe black? Or perhaps something more enjoyable? Sequins? Layers? Something bright? Her clothing has to be appealing from every aspect and in every light. It had to be fancy... but not extravagant. She didn't want to be the actress whose dress choice was mocked the next day online and in the newspaper!

Selena eventually settled on a pearl-grey gown composed of a lovely airy chiffon, with glittering drop earrings that matched her jewelled bodice. It was stylish... yet sparkly. Perfect!

The sun was blazing down on Los Angeles on the afternoon of the event. Photographers yelled Selena's name in an attempt to catch her attention as she stood with her co-stars.

"Selena! Come this way!"

"Selena, please come over here!"

Selena waved and smiled. What a scorcher! In the heat, her jewelled bodice was too tight. But, unlike David and Jake, she wasn't dressed up!

Selena was comforted when the celebs entered the cool of the auditorium. She sat with her on-screen family while each category was presented, along with small snippets from each show.

Mad Men was named Best Drama.

Best Comedy went to 30 Rock.

The Daily Show took home the award for Best Variety Show.

Actors, supporting actors, directors, producers, writers, composers, costume designers, make-up artists, special effects... The list seemed endless.

It was finally time. The nominees for the Outstanding Children's Program award have been announced. Selena squeezed David and Jake's hands on either side of her. Who do you think it is? She didn't dare to take a breath.

'And the prize goes to... Wizards of Waverly Place!'

Selena became giddy with excitement. She was onstage with David, Jake, and the rest of the cast and crew, without knowing how she got there... holding a heavy, golden Emmy award! It was a fantastic sensation. Making the show was a lot of fun. She was overjoyed for everyone who had worked on and supported the program, but especially for the viewers!

Selena's 2009 was shaping up to be a tremendous year. Her career as a singer and actor was taking off... big time.

She had won an Emmy. She'd had a hit album with The Scene. She also appeared in not one, but two new films.

There was Wizards of Waverly Place: The Movie first. Selena travelled to Puerto Rico with the rest of the cast to film. Being away from home with David, Jake, and the rest of her Wizards co-stars felt like a huge family vacation!

Then there came the Princess Protection Program, which was also shot in Puerto Rico. Who is Selena's co-star? Demi Lovato, to be exact. Finally, the best friends were reuniting and playing... best buddies!

Demi, like Selena, was seeking a music career in addition to acting. Don't Forget, her debut album, was released a year before Selena's. The two girls had always wanted to record a duet together, and the Princess Protection Program finally offered them the chance. Their song 'One and the Same' was included on the film's soundtrack.

It was a lot of fun filming with Demi. It was like going back in time, without the enormous purple dinosaur! They shared a hotel, got room service, went out dancing in the evenings, and talked till late at night. They understood one other's deepest secrets; it was like having a sister.

But the filming eventually came to a stop. Demi had to return to Los Angeles to finish her new album. Selena was finishing up her second album with The Scene and getting ready to begin filming the new season of Wizards of Waverly Place.

"We'll see each other back in LA," Selena stated as she hugged her pal goodbye. Demi's limo was waiting for her outside the hotel, ready to transport her to the airport.

"I'll miss you," Demi remarked. "You promise to call me every day?"

"I will keep my promise!"

CHAPTER 10

GENEROUSNESS IN GHANA

Selena stepped out of her automobile into the oppressive heat of central Ghana. Mandy and Brian were her companions. They'd come to see some of the poorest sections in the country, where UNICEF was working to improve the lives of children. Growing up in these conditions was among the most dreadful in the world, with a lack of clean water, food, medicine, and education. Children were dying all throughout the country from diseases that might be readily prevented in other parts of the world.

Selena has been named a UNICEF Goodwill Ambassador. She was the organisation's youngest member at the age of 17, following in the footsteps of David Beckham, Shakira, Robbie Williams, Whoopi Goldberg, and many other well-known figures.When UNICEF contacted Selena, she said yes without hesitation. Being famous provided various rewards, including expensive parties, luxury hotels, limos, and stunning apparel. The list appeared to go on forever. But being able to use her voice to help people who didn't have one was a huge benefit in her new job. Selena wanted to show her audience what life was like for children in locations they had never heard of.

She looked about with wide eyes. Since her arrival yesterday, Selena has spent her entire day in Ghana's capital, Accra. The city centre was densely packed with tall buildings, brightly lit retail centres, and restaurants... It was both fashionable and comfortable. The scenery was completely different.

She had just arrived at a village of around a hundred people who lived in simple red clay homes. Water was pumped from a well; there was no running water in the huts, thus there were no toilets. Children ran about between the huts, playing with toys made from scraps of plastic, twine, and other rubbish. Selena had been warned about poverty, but seeing it first hand was heartbreaking. A happy young lady stood by to meet them.

"Welcome!" she said, shaking Selena's hand.

A small crowd had gathered behind the woman, and others were racing to join them. They were wary of Selena and her family.

"Come on over and say hello!" shouted the lady.

Selena smiled encouragingly.

"Hello, my name is Selena. "Could you please tell me your names?"

They informed her one by one. Selena was relieved that they could talk. Although English was Ghana's official language, she was aware that it was not spoken by everyone in the country. There were almost 250 other languages and dialects spoken here! One of the older girls took a step forward and clasped Selena's hand in hers.

"My baby brother is over there," she added. "Do you want to go and see him?"

The speaker says, "Yes, please!" Selena smiled. She loves babies. She followed the youngster to a little hut where the girl's mother was holding a tiny infant. The baby was adorable. His mother and big sister were clearly thrilled.

"He's eight weeks old," the woman said.

"Only for eight weeks?" "Wow!" remarked Selena. "May I have a cuddle with him?"

"Of course!" the author exclaims. The mother gently placed her sleeping baby into Selena's arms. "You're lucky that he's silent. "Oof! When he sobs!" She sighed, rolling her eyes. Selena's young entourage, on the other hand, was becoming restless. Small hands grabbed at her T-shirt, as questions poured in from all sides.

"Where are you originally from?"

"Do you like Ghana?"

"Come and see our teacher..."

"...our public library..." "...our high school..."

Selena erupted in laughter. "Shhhh! "You're going to startle the baby!"

Selena followed the youngsters as they rushed from hut to hut, calling out to relatives and friends, handing the sleeping infant back to his mother. The locals were bustling everywhere they went. In the neighbouring fields, men and women were gathering crops. Women were cooking and sewing. The sick, including children, were being cared for inside a handful of the shelters by family.

Selena was well aware of how little money they had. "Is there a doctor?" she inquired of her tour guide. "Do people have the medicines they need?"

The guide's response was straightforward. "No. Some of those unwell children will perish if they are not treated immediately." She said that the nearest doctor was an hour's drive away. Medicine was so expensive that few villagers could afford it. It was difficult to hear. Selena and her family had experienced adversity as children, but nothing like this. She had always had enough food. When she was unwell, her parents were always able to provide her with medicine. And, like the majority of youngsters in wealthy countries, she had been immunised against the most common childhood ailments. Children couldn't rely on any of that in this place. She hoped that her work with UNICEF would be beneficial. The charity required funds. They needed people all across the world to understand how their work was directly saving the lives of children.

"Over here!" Selena's boisterous group had proceeded to a long, low building. Its roof was thatched with dried palm fronds, just like the locals' houses. There were no windows in the room. Instead, the building's sides were exposed to the elements.

"This is our school!" says the principal.

The school consisted of a single huge room. Selena inquired, "Where do all the different classes sit?"

"It's one big class," one of the older kids said. "It can be difficult to study at times. The teacher doesn't have much time because he has so many small children to look after."

The teacher appeared at that same moment. The kids flocked around him, sharing their news and asking him questions. Selena could see they liked him a lot. The teacher shook Selena's hand and smiled.

"Not every child can come to school," he said. "These are the fortunate children. Many have to start working at an early age, or stay at home to care for someone who is ill."

Selena reflected on how much she despised going to school. She had always struggled in class and felt foolish. But she realised how fortunate she had been. She had taken her education for granted. These children were desperate for an education, yet many of them may never get one. There were no classes today because it was a Saturday, however...

"We've been working on a song!" The kids couldn't keep their excitement in check any longer. "Can we start singing it now?"

Selena burst out laughing. She turned to face the teacher, who nodded. In an instant, the swarm of raucous students morphed into a well-choreographed choir. They did a series of dance steps to music, a traditional song from the hamlet, with the smallest children standing in front of the bigger ones, while the teacher beat time on a drum. The harmonies were fantastic - some of these youngsters could really sing! A crowd gathered to observe, and everyone soon began to dance. An older woman took Selena's hands in hers and swayed with her to the music. "Not like that... this!" She informed her.

"I've got a lot to learn, haven't I?" Selena burst out laughing.

It had been a fantastic, life-changing day. Will her presence make a difference? Selena realised she had to do everything she could to make it count.

CHAPTER 11

FROM HOLLYWOOD TO HUNGARY

Back in Hollywood, Selena was resolved to do whatever she could to help UNICEF and the incredible work they were doing in Africa and around the world. So, for the second year in a row, she became the spokesperson for the Trick-or-Treat fundraising drive in October 2010. She had helped raise $700,000 the previous year. This year was the campaign's 60th anniversary, and Selena set a lofty goal of $1 million.

"We can do it!" she exclaimed to her fans. "This is your chance. Get involved with me!"

Selena was full of ideas. She created a unique Trick-or-Treat T-shirt. It was doing well and making a lot of money. She also contributed to a charity auction. She was conducting interview after interview, and her social media was ablaze with activity. It felt great to be able to assist. There was even more...

"Selena Gomez and The Scene are performing a benefit concert," Selena said. "On October 26th, here in Los Angeles. "All proceeds will be donated to UNICEF."

Selena rated the concert as one of her favourites thus far. The atmosphere was laid-back, almost festival-like. Selena and her band had just released their second album, A Year Without Rain, and fans were excited to hear a mix of old and new music - 'I Won't Apologise,' 'Naturally,' 'Ghost of You,' 'Intuition' - as well as covers of some of Selena's favourite artists - Pixie Lott's 'Mama Do,' Cheryl Cole's 'Parachute'... The band's songs had a rapid, electric vibe in the studio. But it was fun to perform the songs on a small stage with just a mic and acoustic instruments. It demonstrated how talented her band members were! The most acclaim, however, was reserved for Selena's duet with a young admirer who was picked from the audience to play 'A Year Without Rain' onstage with her idol. Selena's little co-star was spot-on... and the audience went crazy! Selena and her band ended the night with a cover of the iconic song "Magic," to which the audience sang along. It was the ideal way to cap off her maiden acoustic gig.

"We love you, Selena!" said the crowd. Selena was warm and fluffy on the inside. And the best part? It was all for a fantastic cause.

"Your presence here is assisting children all over the world who are far less fortunate than we are," she addressed her fans. "It means everything to me. "I absolutely adore you!"

Selena's goal was to raise $1 million. The UNICEF Trick-or-Treat campaign raised $4 million thanks to her efforts! Selena's social media posts regarding the campaign earned nearly one billion views. It exceeded Selena's expectations and reminded her of something she already knew: her followers were incredible.

Selena was busy learning new film screenplays when she wasn't in the studio creating and recording new music or on set filming Wizards. She had two further films scheduled for 2010: Ramona and Beezus and Monte Carlo. She also had to study for her school exams, working with a tutor. Selena hadn't gone to school in years since her shooting and music schedule was too demanding. But she understood the value of an education. Her journey to Ghana had demonstrated this to her in the most emphatic way possible. Selena was ecstatic about her upcoming films. Ramona and Beezus was based on a children's book series about Ramona, a mischievous little girl, and her big sister. She remembered the books she had read as a child; they were classics! She couldn't wait to see Beezus come to life on the big screen. Monte Carlo couldn't be more dissimilar. Selena played a British teenager who was mistaken for an heiress. She had to learn to speak with a British accent, which wasn't easy...

Fortunately, her Wizards co-star, Gregg Sulkin, played Alex's lover, Mason Greyback.

"You have to help me, Gregg!" Selena pleaded. "And please don't laugh!"

"I'll try not to," Gregg said with a smile. "Let's hear it for what you've got."

"I - like - to - take - tea - with - the - Queen," Selena remarked slowly, her best British accent on display.

"Er, needs a bit of work!" Gregg exclaimed. "Can you try it again?"

"I - like - to - take... I - like - to... I - like - to... Oh, Gregg, I can't do it!" Gregg snorted with delight as Selena burst out laughing.

"You can do it," Gregg said. "But, you know, we don't all talk like the royal family!" "Pay attention to what I'm saying..."

The filming of Monte Carlo took place in Budapest, Hungary, rather than in Monte Carlo. The city charmed Selena: it was like a scene from a fairy tale come to life. She preferred to see the sites at night. The beautiful parliament building on the Danube's brink was illuminated in gold, its reflection sparkling brilliantly in the water. The massive Chain Bridge glittered with hundreds of lights, and Buda Castle, which towered above the city, was a beautiful sight. Selena's phone rapidly became overflowing with images. The narrow cobblestone lanes, the tall, colourful houses, the ornate street lamps... Everything was so old and interesting. She really enjoyed the meal, which included hot goulash and her favourite, pickles! But Selena's most famous sequence in the film was not shot in the picturesque city streets. It was a high school graduation scene in which Selena's character, Grace, and her best friends received their diplomas. Selena had only recently completed her real-life tests. She hadn't had a graduation ceremony because she had been homeschooled, so acting it out on TV was the closest she could get.

"I graduated from high school and got my diploma," she posted on her Facebook page, beside a photo of herself in her gown and mortar board.

Life in Hollywood was strange at times.

OK, do that all the time...

CHAPTER 12

LOVE YOU LIKE A LOVE SONG

Selena and her band were riding high after the success of their first two albums when they returned to Los Angeles. They had a large fan base that was growing with each performance.

They continued on a second tour, performing with some of the world's most popular singers, including Katy Perry, Bruno Mars, and Enrique Iglesias. Selena realised how fortunate they were. Some artists work for years before finding success. However, her label, Hollywood Records, had been there for her band every step of the way. The Scene was back in the studio, working on their third album, When the Sun Goes Down. 'Naturally,' penned by Antonina and Tim, was the best-selling single from Selena's debut album. Antonina and Tim now had a new idea, a song written with songwriter Adam Schmalholz. They played it for Selena at their Santa Monica studio.

Selena's face revealed little as she focused on the lyrics and the melody. But the song had only just begun when Tim and Antonina noticed her foot tapping. Her fingers then began to beat time. She was giggling at the conclusion of the track. "Wow! That was incredible!" "What is its name?"

"'Love You Like a Love Song,' Antonina said."

"We think it's perfect for you," Tim continued.

Selena gave a nod. She did as well. "Can I hear it again?"

This tune was quite catchy! It was already ingrained in her mind. Selena had no question about it. This was her favourite song.

"I love it!" she said to Tim and Antonina. "And I'd love to record it!" says the singer.

By the time they got into the studio with the band and started laying down the music, everyone was convinced that this would be Selena's biggest hit ever. The music was rapid and entertaining. Tim and Antonina suggested a strong, throbbing beat. "It's 'Eurodisco,'" they explained to Selena, who enjoyed the dance ambiance. Selena found herself singing the song as soon as she got up in the morning since it was so seductive. She couldn't help herself! It was a beautiful song, and Selena knew it required an equally extraordinary visual to accompany it. The songs were about falling in love and how strange it felt - perhaps the video should be similarly strange. So Selena enlisted the help of directors Geremy Jasper and Georgie Greville. Their videos were frequently strange, humorous, and thought-provoking. The outcome did not disappoint. Selena attempted to explain it to Mandy.

"I'm singing along to my own song in a Japanese karaoke bar." Then I appear on TV, sitting on a beach with a hippie-looking guy. Then I'm lying on a floating piano in the skies, with a musician dressed as Mozart - it's all quite strange. Next, I'm cruising in space in a car—"

"Stop!" exclaimed Mandy. "It's insane!" I'll have to keep an eye on that..."

Selena burst out laughing. "I haven't gotten to the really weird bit yet."

Her favourite moment involved her standing on a purple field. Ethan and the lads were costumed as a mariachi band, and Selena was swinging a pink lightsaber at a giant heart-shaped pinata.

Yes, this was possibly the most insane thing she'd ever done!

Her fans adored it, as did the song. 'Love You Like a Love Song,' released in June 2011, was Selena's biggest success to date. The reception was incredible when the band performed it live. It had sold over two million copies by the end of the month.

"Two million people have bought our record, you guys!" Selena exclaimed.

They soon had another reason to rejoice: they had won the Teen Choice Awards "Best Love Song" category. Selena Gomez and the Scene played live in front of a star-studded audience before accepting their first music award. Taylor Swift was shouting and clapping her friend in the front row.

And what about alongside her?

Justin Bieber is a megastar singer.

CHAPTER 13

JELENA

Selena was lying on the sofa in Taylor Swift's stunning Los Angeles apartment. Taylor sat cross-legged next to her. A large vase of sweet-smelling flowers, a stack of magazines... and a plate full of chocolate muffins were on the table in front of them. Taylor enjoyed baking.

Selena chose a muffin. "These are amazing," she said as she took a piece. "These are literally the best muffins I've ever had."

"Don't change the subject!" Taylor chastised her companion. "You and Justin... what's going on?"

"Well..." Selena's face lit up with joy. "We're kind of a thing!"

"I knew it!" says the author. Taylor made a squeak. "And, judging by the look on your face, you really like him?"

Selena nodded, her grin widening. "Aw, Taylor, he's amazing. He's certainly cute. He's amusing. He's astute. I've never felt such a connection with somebody before. We're having the nicest time ever!" Taylor embraced Selena and caressed her friend's hair tenderly.

"You know you're not going to be able to hide this forever, don't you?"

Taylor snorted with laughter as Selena grimaced dramatically.

Justin Bieber, a sixteen-year-old Canadian singer, was one of the world's top pop singers. He had millions of followers. They were both aware of Justin's ardent supporters. The Beliebers were not going to be pleased to learn that their idol was involved...

"There are already rumours on social media," Taylor remarked. "Perhaps you should make it official and get it out of the way?"

"We're not ready," Selena admitted. Even without the entire world watching, being an official couple was a huge step! "I mean, who knows what's going to happen," she continued. "I'm still so young." He's even more youthful!" Selena was only eighteen years old, two years younger than Justin.

Selena had witnessed how difficult it was to be in a relationship with another celebrity when she dated Nick Jonas. And no one was as famous as Justin - no one! She didn't want to tell anyone about their connection right now, certainly not the press.

"Plus, if we're official, you'll kick me out of the Lonely Girls Club!" Selena exclaimed to her pal, giving puppy-dog eyes.

The "Lonely Girls Club" consisted of Taylor, Selena, and four other unmarried friends. They met at Taylor's place on a regular basis to talk and eat Taylor's excellent cakes.

"Never!" said Taylor. "There's always a spot for you at the Lonely Girls Club, Selena Gomez."

The rumours regarding Justin and Selena grew stronger over time. Someone created a hashtag on social media: #Jelena. The paparazzi followed Justin and Selena wherever they went. They had to be careful not to hold hands, kiss, or even hug. Within hours, even the simplest gesture of affection would be all over the news. It was extremely difficult!

Finally, while on vacation in St Lucia in January 2011, Selena and Justin let their guard down. They were overjoyed to be together on the gorgeous Caribbean island. How could they not kiss on the beautiful sunlit beach, with the blue water rippling behind them...

The photographs emerged on phones and computer screens all across the world almost instantaneously. Selena and Justin felt it was pointless to try to hide their relationship any longer, so 'Jelena' went public. Their first public appearance as a pair was at the Vanity Fair Oscars party. Then, in May, they attended the Billboard Music Awards, where Justin won Best New Artist. He tried to drag Selena on onstage with him to accept his medal. But she wouldn't allow him... this was his chance! But she received the loudest applause from the audience. Her intelligent, kind-hearted lover deserved to be successful. Many of Justin's admirers were upset to see him with another female, but Jelena had many fans as well. So Justin and Selena chose to bask in their newfound celebrity.

Justin joked on Instagram, posting a photo of himself and Selena as "Brangelina 2.0." Who knew what the future held, and why not have fun imagining?

CHAPTER 14

DREAMS COME TRUE

Selena and Justin's limo came to a stop in front of the Staples Center in downtown Los Angeles. It was LA's largest arena, a prominent music venue, and the home of the famed Los Angeles Lakers basketball team.

"We're getting out here," Justin said.

Blue light poured through the massive glass windows, and the massive red lettering at the top of the skyscraper glowed brightly. However, the stadium was deafeningly quiet. There were no cheering fans. There was no noise from the PA system. There was no one arriving or going.

Selena inquired, "Was there a game tonight?" "Because it appears that we have missed it."

It was getting late. Selena and Justin had spent the evening close, at the Nokia Theater, where Demi Lovato was performing. Demi's new album, Unbroken, had just been released, and she had performed brilliantly. Selena was overjoyed for her pal. In fact, the entire day had been incredible. Selena and Justin had been hanging out in Malibu's Paradise Cove. Selena adored the golden sand, the graceful palm palms, and the limitless blue water. The coast was nearly 250 miles away when I was growing up in Grand Prairie. Her parents had strained to fill the car with enough gas to drive Selena to and from school, let alone take her to the beach. But the beach had become one of Selena's favourite places to visit. If only the photographers would keep their distance!

She'd spotted them hanging around today, as usual, but it hadn't detracted from her delight. She and Justin had strolled hand in hand along the beach in the late-September sunshine, stopping for lunch at the famous Beach Café. Justin was leaving on tour in a few days, and they wanted to spend as much time as possible together. Yes, today was ideal. But why had Justin taken her to a deserted stadium?

"You're not going to sing a concert for me, are you?" she jokingly said.

"It's a surprise," he explained. "Wait and see."

Selena gripped his arm. Justin frequently surprised her with amorous gestures. What could it possibly be? Maybe I'll run into a basketball player? However, the Lakers were not her team. She supported the San Antonio Spurs because she was from Texas. She'd told Justin about it. Did he forget? Justin hustled Selena across Star Plaza to the VIP door as the limo sped away. A guard unlocked the door and led them inside. Then another official appeared.

"My name is Tia," she introduced herself. "Come on this way."

Selena looked around, perplexed. The arena was as quiet inside as it had been outside, but the lights were on and the personnel were on duty...

"Seriously, Justin, what are we doing here?"

Her boyfriend simply smiled inexplicably.

Selena frowned. "You're so irritating, Justin. "Are you aware of that?"

There was no time for dithering. Tia hurried them out of the entryway and along a succession of halls. Some were lined with photographs of Lakers players from the past and present. Some displayed photographs of the artists and bands who had performed at the venue. Tina Turner, Britney Spears, Beyoncé, Rihanna, Taylor Swift, and Lady Gaga... The list went on and on.

"Can't see you anywhere, baby," Selena joked.

"I'm probably too small... "Wait a minute!" Justin discovered his own photograph. "Plenty big enough!"

"No one likes a show-off!"

They appeared to be in the stadium's guts by this point. Tia marched in front of them, occasionally turning around to see if the pair was following her. She eventually pushed through a Personnel only door.

"I think we're in the players' area," Selena said quietly. She noticed a sign directing her to the home team's locker room. She wasn't sure why she was keeping her voice down - they didn't seem to be supposed to be here!

Tia turned a sharp corner. The walls and the floor were now composed of concrete. Their footfalls were louder than usual, and the air seemed colder. Was this the entrance of the players? Tia pushed open a double door, and Selena and Justin entered. They were plunged into darkness when the doors slammed shut behind them.

But only for a moment...

A thousand bulbs lit up with a quick buzz and sizzle. The massive stadium was suddenly lit up. The big and gleaming basketball court stretched out in front of them. Row after row of seats reached the ceiling. The massive screen above the centre of the court glowed in a spectrum of colours.

And there wasn't another soul in the arena. Tia had also magically vanished.

Selena cupped her hand over her mouth. "You didn't...!"

"My dear lady..." Justin took her hand and proceeded to walk her across the court. Selena only needed a split second to notice where he was going.

"Justin! This is excessive!"

At the far end of the court, there was a white-clothed table and two chairs. Selena noticed flowers, gleaming silver tableware, and clean white tablecloths. Dinner! She suddenly realised how hungry she was.

"This is completely surreal!" exclaimed Selena as she wrapped her arms around her boyfriend. "I love it, thank you!"

Someone, somewhere, was keeping an eye on them, because as soon as they sat down, a waiter emerged, bringing drinks and a starter, followed by steak and chips placed on a silver tray. Even by Justin's standards, this was a romantic gesture off the charts! The lights suddenly darkened, and a melancholy music filled the stadium. The enormous screen above the court was lit up with sepia images. A massive ship. Crowds waving on board and on the quayside... then a picture of the vast blue water... and... Titanic! It was Selena's favourite film, and it was also one of the most romantic films ever filmed. Justin moved in for a kiss, and this time no one was looking. There will be no paparazzi. There are no cameras. For once, they were absolutely alone in the centre of a 20,000-seat stadium.

CHAPTER 15

WORLD TOUR

While, off-screen, Selena was happily in love with a pop megastar, on-screen in Wizards of Waverly Place, her character Alex wasn't so lucky. If she didn't win the competition to become the Family Wizard, she would have to say goodbye – forever – to her boyfriend, Mason Greenback, the werewolf. It would be a howling shame.

The final episode of the final series of Wizards aired on 6 January, 2012. With nearly 10 million viewers, it was the most-watched series finale in the history of the Disney Channel. The fans were on the edge of their seats. What would happen to the characters they had come to love? Would Alex win and stay with Mason? Or would her brothers beat her to victory? Anything was possible!

The actors had filmed the final scenes months before. Selena and her fellow cast members had managed to keep the plot a secret ever since – they couldn't even tell their families!

Selena could hardly believe that Wizards was coming to an end. It had been such a special experience, working with such talented actors, directors and crew. On the final day of filming, the whole team laughed and cried together. How much they would miss this colourful, friendly world!

Selena, Jake and David were backstage chatting with the production team when the director called them over. The crew had gathered round. "We've got presents for you," said the director, handing each of them a parcel. "Open them!"

Selena pulled the paper from her parcel. Whatever was inside was long and thin. Could it be...?

"My wand!" gasped Selena. "Thank you."

Selena had held this wand so many times that it almost felt like a piece of her. It was the perfect souvenir of a magical time.

"I'm going to frame it," she declared – but not before giving it one final wizard's flourish.

It was sad to say goodbye to Wizards, but Selena Gomez – actor, singer, teen idol – was busier than ever. Her fans still knew her best as Alex Russo, but Selena was determined to rebrand herself as a grown-up singer and movie star.

The first step? Spring Breakers. It was her first "grown-up" movie and had been so much fun to make, acting alongside rising stars Ashley Benson, Rachel Korine and Vanessa Hudgens. It was also the biggest production Selena had been involved in so far. For weeks, the beach town of St Petersburg, Florida, had been taken over by actors and film crew. Selena and her co-stars had enjoyed acting alongside real college students on their spring break, who provided the crowd scenes.

And then there was Selena's new album, Stars Dance. Finally, after three albums with The Scene, Selena had decided to go solo. She would miss her talented band, but this was a new beginning and she was excited. Up till now, music had felt like a sort of 'professional hobby'. She had thought of herself as an actress who liked to sing. But now it is getting serious... Once the album was released, Selena would be going on her first solo tour – a world tour!

Her record label believed in her. Her fans believed in her. But Selena herself couldn't help having doubts. Could she pull it off? Could she make it as a "proper" singer? One very famous pop star seemed to think so... Selena was onstage with Ashley and Rachel at a press conference to promote Spring Breakers. The actors faced a room full of reporters asking questions. Selena had done many press interviews so far in her career. The questions were usually predictable, almost too easy. But then a voice from the back of the room piped up: "Ladies, did you lip-sync to Britney Spears? You lip-synced, right?"

The scene that the reporter was referring to was set in a bar, where the girls sang their version of Britney's 'Hit Me Baby One More Time'. Selena bristled with indignation. How dare he! Lip-syncing was the worst crime a singer could be accused of...

But she chose to laugh instead. "No lip-syncing," she declared. "Do you want the proof?"

She began to sing the opening notes of the song.

Ashley and Rachel looked at each other. Was this really happening? A live Britney Spears karaoke, at a press conference?

A helpful producer projected the lyrics onto the screen behind them. OK, it was happening! A little nervously, Ashley and Rachel joined in.

"No lip-syncing, I think you'll agree!" laughed Selena when they came to the end of the song.

It wasn't long before a video of the impromptu performance was uploaded to Twitter – and Britney saw it. She posted her response: she loved it. The superstar even suggested a duet!

Selena's heart was in her mouth. She had just been tweeted by her idol! She replied straight away: My life is made!

Getting praise from her favourite singer felt amazing. It was the confidence boost Selena needed before setting off on her first world tour. Now she knew she could do it. After all, Britney had told her so!

In mid-August, Selena said goodbye to her friends and family and boarded the first of many planes. She was bound for a new city, a new country and the first performance of her Stars Dance show. The tour started in Canada, before heading to Europe and the Middle East, then back to the US, followed by Asia and Australia. She would be on tour for seven months.

Selena loved performing live. Her audience meant everything to her; the energy and adrenaline she got from them was like nothing else. Seeing how her fans reacted to her songs – it was the best feeling in the world.

She and her team had put together a show that focused on singing and dancing. She didn't want complicated staging. Apart from her backing singers, there was just a screen playing videos. One of them showed Selena opening a gift box containing the famous sparkly microphone that she always used, with her name written on it in crystals. Via a series of shots of flashing cameras and swirling newspaper headlines, she showed her fans how hard it was to live under the constant gaze of the media. Selena had been a celebrity for most of her life – but she was still figuring it out.

Seeing the world was a dream come true for Selena, particularly visiting Europe. Climbing the Eiffel Tower. Staring up at Big Ben. Wandering round the canals of Amsterdam. Plus Stockholm, Vienna, Oslo... She had been nervous about feeling lonely on tour, but many of her friends came out to visit her: Hollywood friends and friends from Texas too. Selena had kept in touch with girls she'd known since third grade.

And when she wasn't performing or sightseeing, Selena spent hours on Skype and ichat, catching up with friends and family back in the US. She spoke to Mandy every day.

"Mom! How are you? How's Gracie?"

Gracie was Selena's new baby sister, born just a few months earlier to Mandy and Brian. Selena adored her tiny half-sister.

"We're all doing well, honey. Gracie's asleep." Mandy angled her tablet to show the serene face of her sleeping daughter. "Look – how gorgeous is that!"

Selena felt her heart melting in her chest. A wave of homesickness rushed over her. "I wish I could spend more time there with you, Mom," she said.

"I know, honey. But you're on such a big adventure. Where are you today?"

"Milan!" Selena grinned. "It's crazy. Everyone's so stylish. Even the dogs are stylish! And the food is incredible."

"You look tired though, sweetie. Are you getting enough rest?" Mandy noticed how pale Selena looked. There were dark circles round her eyes.

"There's no time, Mom."

It was true. Preparing for a concert took most of the day. Then, in the evening, Selena spent two hours onstage. Her setlist had twenty songs on it.

"I'm OK, Mom, honestly."

But Mandy was concerned. Her daughter often pushed herself too hard. She wished she was there to look after her.

"Try to take it easy, Selena," Mandy told her. "Promise me?"

"I promise, Mom. Don't worry."

CHAPTER 16

TIME OUT

But by the end of the year, calamity had struck.

Tokyo has been cancelled.

Shanghai has been cancelled.

Singapore has been cancelled.

Perth has been cancelled.

Sydney has been cancelled.

Melbourne has been cancelled.

The list seemed endless. Selena's admirers across Asia and Australia were disappointed to find that the concerts they had been looking forward to would not take place. Selena was not going to show up.

Selena apologised on her website. She disliked disappointing her fans.

She wrote, "I need to spend some time on myself in order to be the best person I can be." I hope you understand how much each of you means to me.

Her fans were heartbroken and concerned. Was Selena unwell? What was the situation?

The truth was that Selena had no idea. She was completely fatigued. It wasn't just tired; it was more. The life of a singer and actor was never easy. This was unique. Selena could barely get out of bed on some days.

She went to one doctor, then another, and another. They all had tests, but it took a year for Selena and her family to find out...

Selena was afflicted with lupus.

The immune system in most people's bodies works to safeguard and maintain the body's health. Lupus, on the other hand, leads the immune system to fight the body rather than protect it. Selena's body was assaulting itself from the inside out. Lupus patients who do not have a functioning immune system can become very unwell very quickly - and lupus was rendering Selena vulnerable to illnesses that most people's bodies can readily fight.

What is the solution? Selena and her family were astounded to discover that there were none. Selena's doctor recommended chemotherapy, which would render her unable to work for several months. Selena agreed to the procedure. However, the sickness would always be present. Lupus was a chronic illness that would not go away.

"The most important thing for you to do is to take it easy," Selena's doctor advised. "You need to get plenty of rest. You don't get enough."

It was correct. But Selena was terrified. Her career was extremely important to her. She did not want to pass up opportunities. Most importantly, she didn't want to let her admirers down again.

"You're going to have to be tough with yourself," the doctor said emphatically. "Put it this way - if you get really sick, you won't be able to work at all..."

Selena forced herself to unwind when the final leg of her tour was cancelled. She made a decision: she would take time out whenever she needed it, regardless of the circumstances. It was difficult not to feel sorry for herself at times; most 21-year-olds were not concerned about their health. But she'd make do with what she had. She would deal with her sickness and not let it hold her back.

Selena improved her lupus management skills over the weeks and months that followed. Taking it easy did not come naturally to her, but she learned to recognize when she needed one. She discovered that with careful planning, she could perform, record, act - and rest.

She was finally able to return to the spotlight.

It was the month of April of 2013.

Selena was back onstage and looking fantastic. She was scheduled to perform at the MTV Music Awards tonight. She glanced out at a star-studded audience set to hear her new song 'Come and Get It' for the first time.

Wow! Was it Channing Tatum up front? And what about Brad Pitt? Selena experienced a surge of nerves. What was she doing here, surrounded by Hollywood A-listers? She felt like a fraud!

But as soon as the music started, Selena's adrenaline started pumping. She pushed herself into the dance routines, tossing her hair. She was precisely where she needed to be, onstage! Selena had finally said good-by to her old Disney persona. Her new outfit was bold and confident, consisting of an elegantly shredded red dress, a sparkling crimson bindi, black eye shadow, and gold ballet heels. She finally felt like the "proper" vocalist she had always wanted to be.

She was applauded as she exited the stage. 'Come and Get It' was a big smash! Selena flung herself into a chair in her dressing room. Finally, a chance to unwind! Or not... Selena was startled when she heard a short, sharp knock on the door.

"Come on in," she said.

The young backstage runner appeared ecstatic.

She exclaimed, "Brad Pitt wants to meet you!" "He's waiting for you downstairs."

Selena's pupils dilated. Really?! A meeting with one of the world's most famous actors? But, why?

"Shall I show him up?" inquired the runner.

"Er, yeah." I suppose. Wow!"

"We'll be right back in two minutes."

Selena became terrified as soon as the door was shut. This can't be happening, can it? She suddenly didn't feel like a "proper" vocalist. She wanted to run away. She dove under the table, put her face into her knees, and remained there for a minute, till her heart slowed down. Take a few deep breaths! Selena had crawled out from behind the table by the time her guest arrived. Cool. Calm. Poised.

"Selena! That was an incredible performance." Brad smiled heartily as he shook her hand. "May I take a photo with you?" My children are huge fans of your show!"

It was impossible to avoid the Wizards of Waverly Place. Selena would always remain Alex Russo to some fans, including the Pitt family! Brad smiled as he removed his phone from his pocket, and Selena's cool exterior shattered. She took out her phone. "Can I get a picture too?" she enquired. She felt like a child again. Mr. Brad Pitt! It couldn't get any bigger than this!

CHAPTER 17

THE HEART WANTS WHAT IT WANTS

Selena stood in front of a huge mirror in the middle of a beautiful dressing room. On the table in front of her was a jumble of perfume bottles, make-up, hair spray and several big vases of flowers.

It looked real... but it wasn't. It was the set of Selena's new music video. The song? 'The Heart Wants What It Wants'.

Selena stared into the mirror. For an instant, a doubt came into her head. Did she really want to do this, make her innermost feelings public for the whole world to hear?

The feeling quickly disappeared.

"I'm ready," she told her producers, Tim and Antonina. "I'm just speaking normally, right?"

There was a microphone taped under the table. Antonina reached to switch it on.

"Yes, normal volume," she told her. "The mic will pick up everything, and we'll edit it afterwards."

"I'm not sure what I'm going to say. I might talk nonsense."

"It doesn't matter," said Tim. "Just speak from the heart. Imagine we're not here. No cameras. No mic. You're all alone."

They stepped away, and Selena began to speak. She thought it would be hard, but actually it was easy. In her mind, the production crew faded away. It was just her, talking to herself – and to Justin.

Since their incredible date at the Staples Center, Jelena's relationship had been a rollercoaster: on and off again more times than their fans could keep track of. But this time, Selena felt sure it was over for good. And it hurt so much. Selena began to speak – and suddenly the words came flooding out. Her fingers gripped the edge of the dressing table, and tears rolled down her cheeks. Somehow, though, it felt good to speak her heartbreak out loud.

"Wow," said Antonina when Selena stopped speaking. "That was really powerful, really honest. Are you OK?"

Selena nodded. Reliving her break-up with Justin was the hardest thing ever – but it had been good for her. She felt lighter.

And now she had to focus again. "Over to you. Work your magic!" she said. She knew that just a few seconds of the conversation she had just recorded would be used on the final video. "And please don't make me sound too crazy!"

The song itself had been recorded a few months earlier. Selena and her producers agreed: 'The Heart Wants What It Wants' was her best song yet. Selena had co-written it, and she knew the world would guess instantly that it was about Justin. So why not add her own words, spoken from her heart? Selena wasn't scared of her fans seeing who she was. Be emotionally honest – that was her mantra, how she wanted to live. And she wanted to help her fans to do the same.

Another day, another change of clothes... But this time was different.

Selena Gomez was spotted backstage at the American Music Awards. She was set to perform 'The Heart Wants What It Wants' for the first time live. Taylor's best buddy would be there, cheering her on.

"Fifteen minutes, Selena," the backstage runner said.

"Thanks," Selena replied.

She attempted to sound lively, but her voice came out choked. The dressing room was crowded with hairdressers, make-up artists, and other professionals. The air was alive with conversation and laughing. Selena examined herself in the mirror. She tried to grin, but her eyes returned blankly. The noise in the room and the brightness of the lights became uncomfortable.

Selena hurried out of the room and down the corridor without putting on her shoes. She made her way to the restroom, the only place she knew she could be alone.

She locked herself in a cubicle after fumbling for the lock. She collapsed against the door and dropped to the ground slowly. Selena sat with her head on her knees and closed her eyes.

And cried.

The strain was excruciating.

It wasn't her admirers. It was never her admirers. Her admirers got it. It was everyone else's desire for her to be this or that. Do this and that. Declare this, declare that... She worked so hard all the time to please everyone!

Mandy's words came into Selena's thoughts as she sat on the floor, tears streaming down her face: she needed to trust herself. She had to take charge!

Selena rose slowly. She knew what she had to do when she got out of the toilet.

She didn't care what everyone else thought anymore. Her friends, her fans, and herself were the only people who cared.

The runner exclaimed, "Two minutes!"

There was terror in the changing room by the time Selena reappeared. Her team had realised she was no longer with them. But the celebrity remained calm. She brushed her hair, reapplied her smudged mascara, and made her way to the stage.

'Everyone, stand up for Selena Gomez!'

Onstage, Selena stood in the shadows. Emotions whirled within her. She wished she could open her mouth and sing. She felt the most in control while she was singing.

The quiet was broken when the first notes of 'The Heart Wants What It Wants' were heard in the room. For the first time, the audience heard pieces of a terrible talk regarding Justin.

A massive video screen lit up behind Selena. The screen was filled with images of barbed wire, smashed glass, and red rose petals scattered like drops of blood.

Selena started singing. Her voice was smooth and rich. Her eyes were wet with tears. She sang with all her heart, and nothing else in the world mattered. Neither did her audience. She was only singing to herself.

Finally, the image displayed light breaking through the clouds, followed by wings spreading open and soaring into the air. Hope had triumphed over darkness and pain.

Selena took a deep breath and lowered her head.

She'd never sung anything like this before. There was a brief moment of stillness before the applause began. Taylor was noticed in the audience by Selena. Her friend was also in tears!

Selena realised that was the first time she had been fully, completely, 100% herself.

CHAPTER 18

TAKING CONTROL

"I've got a project for you," Taylor explained. "Would you like to try something completely new?"

The girls had returned to Taylor's flat. Of course, there was cake, and Taylor and Selena were discussing new beginnings.

"Is this a new project?" "Bring it on!" exclaimed Selena.

She was eager to find out what her friend had in mind.

"I'd like to make an epic video for 'Bad Blood.'" "Something unique." Taylor's latest single, 'Bad Blood,' featured Kendrick Lamar. "And I want you to be in it."

Selena grinned. "Cool. "I'm up for it!"

"But here's the thing. I want youtube to be the polar opposite of Selena. I want you to be the badass antagonist. My adversary."

Taylor explained the plot.

"I'm Catastrophe, a superhero, and you're my crime-fighting partner." We just beat the group of thugs, yet you betray me. You throw me out the window... "Does that sound good?"

"Sounds cool," Selena responded, smiling.

"I'm hurt, but I meet a group of girls who look after me - and we plot revenge on you." You also have a bunch of girls you've groomed to take me out. By the way, I believe this is all set in London. The eventual result is a massive stalemate. We punch each other, causing a massive explosion. "What are your thoughts?"

"Wow. "I'm at a loss for words."

"Say yes!" exclaimed Taylor.

"Yes, OK! Yes!"

"There's even more..."

"I thought there might be." Selena grinned as she saw how happy her friend was.

Taylor was almost shrieking at this point. "Now that I've got you on board, I'm going to get a lot more." Serayah, Cara Delevigne, Jessica Alba, Lena Dunham, Cindy Crawford... you get to name your character!'

It sounded fantastic. Taylor did an incredible job with everything she accomplished. Selena recognized how fortunate she was to have such a wise, caring, and inspiring friend in her life. When you have pals like Taylor, who needs a boyfriend?

Selena had made the decision to take charge of her life, and she was doing so. Her record label was the first to change. She'd been with Hollywood Records since she was sixteen, when they initially signed her. Lady Gaga's new label was Interscope, which also housed Katy Perry, Ellie Goulding, Madonna, and many other prominent artists.

Then there was her boss... Mandy and Brian had been Selena's managers when she first appeared on Barney. But the moment had come to separate family and business. She desired to be herself.

Selena would continue to collaborate with Mandy. Netflix had acquired the rights to make the 13 Reasons Why TV version, with Mandy serving as an executive producer. Selena was now too old to play the lead, but she would work as an executive producer alongside her mother. It was a thrilling opportunity for her to attempt something new - her first part on the other side of the camera!

She also left the lovely Los Angeles home she shared with Mandy and Brian. Selena desired to be self-sufficient. She shared a chic apartment with her friend Francia Rasa. Francia was also an actor, and Selena appreciated being able to discuss the joys and tribulations of her job with someone who understood. The two girls had a great time living together.

And the changes appeared to be working. Selena was feeling more confident and creative than she had in a long time...

CHAPTER 19

MEXICO

A brilliant pink and gold sunset spilled across the horizon. Palm trees swayed against the sky, silhouetted. Selena rested in a hammock in a peaceful nook of Puerto Vallarta, away from the nightlife, listening to the sounds of the evening.

The waves lapped gently. The movement of palm fronds. The insects' high-pitched chirp. The odd thrum of an engine as a scooter navigated the cobblestone streets.

Selena had so many mixed feelings about this community. There was the incredible New Year's Eve she'd spent here with Justin, relaxing by the pool beneath the stars. A year later, their relationship ended here. There was the holiday a few months ago when paparazzi photographed her in a swimsuit and the world's media body-shamed her. Her fury was still fresh in her mind... Who dares to criticise her body?

But right now, when the sky went from pink to blue and the first stars appeared, Selena was content. Her house was in Los Angeles. Her birthplace was Texas. Her roots, however, were in Mexico. She felt at home here.

"Can you hear that music?" Selena inquired, turning to face her pals.

A solitary guitar sound emerged above the surrounding noises. In the neighbourhood tavern, a band was performing. Selena's favourite aspect of Mexico was its music. She enjoyed the ancient rhythms, as well as the fire and enthusiasm. Every song presented a story of love and heartbreak, bravery and adventure.

Selena felt most creative while she was here, which is why she chose to bring her production crew to this seaside property. She hoped they'd write some fantastic songs away from the buzz and bustle of Los Angeles.

And, of course, it was enjoyable to hang around!

Her producers, Tim and Antonina, the rapper and producer Hit-Boy, and two songwriters, Justin Tranter and Julia Michaels, were all there. Tim and Antonina had brought recording gear and turned the smallest bedroom into a mini-studio. The entire group could barely fit into the room, but Selena felt more at ease here than in the enormous studio in Los Angeles. Every morning, she awoke giddy with enthusiasm. She was certain that incredible things would occur.

"And, hey, it's nice to be here with people I won't have an epic bust-up with," she jokingly added.

The audience laughed.

"How is Justin?" Tim inquired.

"He's been seeing someone."

For a brief period, there was silence.

"I'll always care about him," Selena said. "He was my very first love." I want him to be content."

Justin's friendship meant everything to her, and she knew he felt the same way. She missed him, and the media was continually spreading rumours that they were reuniting. But they were better as friends, she reasoned.

"So, what exactly do you want the new album to say?" Antonina inquired. She was expecting Selena to have a vision.

"I want to write about the pressure to be perfect," said Selena. "It's not only me who feels this way. It affects all young people, famous or not."

Her companions nodded. They were all aware of how difficult Selena's continual media attention was for her.

Selena went on. "I want to show how I got through that." I'd like to state unequivocally that rage and resentment are not the solution. It is love and kindness. And trust. "I want to write about everything that helps me."

Selena looked up at the sky, which had turned velvety dark and glittered with thousands of stars. She realised how fortunate she was to have this amazing work. It was an honour to be able to speak up and know that millions of people were listening.

"I want these songs to be a reflection of me," she explained. "I'm not scared to be myself anymore."

Genuineness, faith, love, and kindness. The themes hung in the air, while the guitar continued to play in the distance.

"I have an idea," Selena remarked. She began to hum the opening few notes of a song. "I think it might be the start of something..."

The song was recorded by five o'clock in the morning. It's called 'Body Heat.'

Selena and her pals sat over the recording deck in the little makeshift studio, clutching mugs of coffee to keep them awake. They'd been awake for 17 hours.

Antonina said, "We did it!"

Selena grinned. She was high on caffeine and adrenaline. The melody she had sung from her hammock a few hours before had grown into a whole recording, complete with lyrics and instrumentals. The guitar had found a home at the beginning of the song. A trumpet, a saxophone, and a traditional Mexican horn had been added. The flavour was really Mexican.

Inspiration had struck, and the right individuals had arrived at precisely the right time.

"You guys are amazing," Selena said. "Thank you so much for making this happen!"

From that day forward, in Mexico, then back in LA, the songs kept coming: 'Hands to Myself.'

'Well done.'

'Same Old Love,' 'Kill 'Em with Kindness'.

The last one was especially meaningful to Selena, as it was inspired by her own experience with body-shaming.

"If I can help just one person who has been made to feel bad about their body, making this album will be worth it," she told Tim and Antonina one day in the Los Angeles studio.

"One person?" Antonina grinned. "On Instagram alone, you have over a hundred million followers." You'll benefit a lot more people than that!"

The album's title was chosen by Selena. That's exactly how it felt. She had discovered so much about herself in the previous year. She felt like a new, stronger, and better version of herself. What about the music? That sounded strange as well. Tim, Antonina, and the rest of the crew had worked tirelessly to give Selena a distinct new sound. Selena had hoped for a rich and sultry outcome, and she got it. She hoped that her fans would feel the same way as she did as she waited for the album to be released!

CHAPTER 20

REVIVAL

Revival was released in October of this year. The reception was fantastic. Selena's new sound and her insightful, impassioned lyrics were praised by both fans and reviewers. Selena was overjoyed. She had written and sung from the bottom of her heart. She was overjoyed that her fans got it!

What's the next stop? A tour.

The Revival tour had been planned for months. Selena would travel across North America, Asia, Australia and New Zealand, Europe, the Middle East, and South America between May and December. Joe Jonas' band, DNCE, served as her opening act.

Joe had been in her life for quite some time. In Wizards of Waverly Place, he auditioned for the role of Justin, Selena's on-screen brother. Of course, he dated Taylor Swift and Demi Lovato. Selena still made fun of Joe's awful Central Park date with Taylor and his brother Nick.

"You've dated both of my best friends," Selena remarked one day. "Maybe we should..."

Joe appeared stunned. "Oh, no." Way too strange." He made a shaky motion with his head. "No... Selena... I..."

"I'm kidding! "Your mug!"

Selena was well aware that she would miss Taylor and Demi while she was abroad. But she and Joe got along great. It'd be fantastic to hang out with him and his band as they travelled to new locations, stayed in luxurious hotels, and worked tirelessly to put on the best show yet. Selena had made it clear that Revival would be nothing like Stars Dance. There'd be more spectacle, excitement, props, and wardrobe changes. Selena was confident that she could command the stage even more powerfully than previously. There was a heavy Mexican influence, with Day of the Dead masks included. Selena had also decided to demonstrate her aptitude for playing the piano... live. It would be a tragedy if her anxiety suddenly took over! But it was worth the risk since Selena, as usual, wanted to push herself. The tour began in Las Vegas on a sunny spring evening. Selena could see all the splendour and glamour of Vegas as her chauffeur drove her through traffic towards the Mandalay Bay Events Center: the gorgeous Bellagio fountain, the brilliant Eiffel Tower, the Statue of Liberty, the Great Pyramid, the Venetian palace... It was like taking a world tour in a single limo journey! Selena's entire body tingles with anticipation. Vegas was incredible. She was ecstatic to be onstage.

But there were still hours until the concert. Selena sat calmly as stylists glossed and volumized her long brown hair, and make-up professionals meticulously accentuated her features with smokey black eyeliner, mascara, and a deep, velvety lipstick. Finally, she was helped into her first costume: a sheer, black, sequin-strewn bodysuit.

The audience stretched as far as Selena's eyes could see from the stage in the darkness. The only lights in the stadium were the dazzling dots of phone displays, which seemed like a blanket of stars stretching for miles. But the applause was electric. Her admirers! There are over ten thousand of them! Selena's heart went out to everyone who had come to show her support. She was hoping they could sense it!

The final song, 'Revival,' was the show's high point. Sparks erupted from the stage's sides like fireworks, followed by massive clouds of smoke that glowed pink and blue under the lights. Pink light beams flashed across the stadium as showers of coloured confetti fell on the audience. Finally, Selena could see the joy and excitement on her fans' faces as they raised their arms in the air, dancing and swaying to her song.

"Thank you so much, Las Vegas!" she exclaimed. As she hurried offstage, her heart was beating. What a fantastic first night it had been.

And now what? The same show, repeated 90 times!

The next day, Selena and her production crew, singers, and dancers were back on the road, with coaches and lorries full of costumes, props, and scenery. They visited Fresno, Sacramento, San Jose, and Seattle. Then it was on to Canada, then back to the US for six weeks before arriving in Quebec City. Then they travelled long-distance to Indonesia to begin the Asian part of the tour. Audiences erupted in every location and venue as Selena gave her tremendous performance.

But fatigue was weighing Selena down. She was giving three or four concerts per week. Joe was apprehensive by the time they arrived in Tokyo, their final Asian destination.

"Selena! Selena! Selena!" He had knocked on her hotel room door for the third time. "The automobile has arrived. "Didn't you want to see the sights?"

Selena pushed open the door. He could tell she had been crying because she was still in her pyjamas.

"I've tried calling you," Joe said. "You didn't pick up."

"I apologise. "I couldn't do it."

"You're shaking!" Joe clasped Selena's hand in his. It was shaking. "Selena, have a seat. "Please explain what's going on."

"I believe I had a panic attack." I couldn't take a breath. I tried calling, but... it... just..." The words just wouldn't come out. Selena covered her face with her hands. Her entire body shook.

"It's OK. It's alright, Selena."

"I can't do it," she said quietly.

"The show?"

She gave a nod. Tears streamed down her face.

Joe realised what was going on. Selena's Lupus symptoms were exhaustion, anxiety, and sadness. "We can cancel the show, you know," he added tentatively. If necessary, the entire tour. It's not the end of the world."

But it only made Selena sob louder. She couldn't do it! She disliked disappointing her fans.

Joe encircled her with his arms. "Consider it. I'll be there for you no matter what."

The show went on. Selena appeared at the Tokyo International Forum the following day. No one would have known her inner uneasiness as she strided boldly across the stage in her shimmering gold bodysuit. She only burst into tears again when she returned to her dressing room and locked the door.

She didn't know how she was going to go on.

Finally, in August, Selena decided to take some time off. She'd done 55 concerts in 100 days. She had pushed herself to the limit. Any additional delay could have disastrous consequences.

Selena cancelled the second leg of her tour, Europe, Saudi Arabia, and South America, with regret and despair, but knowing she was doing the right thing. She was especially depressed about Mexico. She hadn't performed there since her previous tour with The Scene in 2012. Revival's final destination would have been Guadalajara. She was aware of how special it would have been to conclude the tour in her spiritual home.

So Selena rested once again. It was very frustrating to see Joe and his band return to the LA studio and know she couldn't. But her health was deteriorating. She couldn't do anything else. And she made a choice. The earnings from the Revival tour would be donated to the Alliance for Lupus Research. Perhaps one day there will be a cure for this crippling condition. Selena made an exception to her relaxing rule in November 2016, when she appeared at the star-studded American Music Awards. She was nominated for the prestigious award for Favorite Pop/Rock Female Artist. It was an award chosen by popular vote. Selena triumphed against Rihanna, Adele, Taylor Swift, and others. And she realised that none of it mattered - health difficulties, a few months away from the spotlight. Her 125 million followers simply wanted her to be herself. It was her honesty about all of that that made her powerful - and unique. Standing onstage to accept the prize, Selena reflected on her dramatic performance of 'The Heart Wants What It Wants' at the same event two years ago.

"In 2014," she reminded her audience, "here on this stage was the first time that I was authentically one hundred percent honest with all of you."

She informed them she was broken inside at the time. But not any longer.

"If you are broken," she went on, "you do not have to stay broken."

The applause was raucous. Her friends and fans all understood how hard she had worked to reclaim control of her career, health, and life... It was extremely inspirational to witness.

CHAPTER 21

A FOREVER FRIEND

Surgeons with masks and scrubs bent anxiously over the bodies of two young ladies in different operating rooms at Cedars Sinai Hospital in Los Angeles.

Selena Gomez was one of them. Francia Raisa, Selena's friend and flatmate, was the other. Selena was having kidney transplant surgery. She had been brought to the hospital a month before with kidney failure caused by her persistent condition, lupus. Her donor was Francia. She was donating one of her kidneys to save the life of a friend.

The transplant procedure was supposed to last two hours, but there was a complication: a ruptured artery. A vein in Selena's leg would have to be removed and used to build a new artery to replace the injured one. Selena's new kidney would not stay in place without it, and she could die on the operating table. Additional surgery could take up to six hours. The surgeons worked meticulously, as Mandy waited for news elsewhere in the hospital.

Francia expected to see her friend when she awoke from anaesthesia. But where had she gone? What had happened to Selena? Mandy elaborated. Selena was not yet safe. They'd have to wait and hope.

Francia and Selena had known each other for nine years, and as Selena's flatmate, Francia had witnessed her friend's health deteriorate every day. Selena was exhausted and weak. She'd barely had the energy to open a bottle of water on a particularly awful day.

Selena then stated that she had gone for some testing one day.

"My doctors say I need a new kidney," Selena explained to a friend. "Without it, I'll get sicker and sicker." However, the waiting list is seven to ten years long." Her eyes were filled with tears.

A replacement kidney? Francia was well aware of the magnitude of the operation. Patients were forced to wait for the appropriate kidney to be given. A non-matching kidney would be rejected by the patient's body.

Francia didn't have to think about it.

"I'll get tested," she said flatly. "Right away." I'll give you one of my kidneys if I can!"

Selena objected because it was such a large sacrifice, but Francia was adamant. Selena was like a sister to her. She couldn't face the thought of her pal in pain. It was conceivable to live a perfectly normal life with only one kidney.

The results were available within a few days. It was the outcome Francia had hoped for. She was a perfect match! Before each operation, a potential organ donor must pass dozens of tests. Blood testing, diabetes tests, a CT scan, X-rays... Mental and emotional well-being must also be assessed. Normally, the process would take months. But Selena's health was rapidly deteriorating - it was an emergency. Francia completed all of the tests in one day. The date of the operation was set.

Francia returned home a few days later to find Selena had prepared a surprise for her. Her buddy presented her with a gift that was nicely wrapped in coloured paper and ribbons. Francia removed the paper to see a box shaped like a bible, a symbol of their shared faith. Their special friendship motto was engraved on the top: "A sister is a forever friend." A kidney bean was found inside the packaging. Francia couldn't decide whether to laugh or cry since she was both happy and afraid. Surgeons with masks and scrubs bent anxiously over the bodies of two young ladies in different operating rooms at Cedars Sinai Hospital in Los Angeles.

Selena Gomez was one of them. Francia Raisa, Selena's friend and flatmate, was the other. Selena was having kidney transplant surgery. She had been brought to the hospital a month before with kidney failure caused by her persistent condition, lupus. Her donor was Francia. She was donating one of her kidneys to save the life of a friend. The transplant procedure was supposed to last two hours, but there was a complication: a ruptured artery. A vein in Selena's leg would have to be removed and used to build a new artery to replace the injured one. Selena's new kidney would not stay in place without it, and she could die on the operating table. Additional surgery could take up to six hours. The surgeons worked meticulously, as Mandy waited for news elsewhere in the hospital.

Francia expected to see her friend when she awoke from anaesthesia. But where had she gone? What had happened to Selena? Mandy elaborated. Selena was not yet safe. They'd have to wait and hope.

Francia and Selena had known each other for nine years, and as Selena's flatmate, Francia had witnessed her friend's health deteriorate every day. Selena was exhausted and weak. She'd barely had the energy to open a bottle of water on a particularly awful day.

Selena then stated that she had gone for some testing one day.

"My doctors say I need a new kidney," Selena explained to a friend. "Without it, I'll get sicker and sicker." However, the waiting list is seven to ten years long." Her eyes were filled with tears.

A replacement kidney? Francia was well aware of the magnitude of the operation. Patients were forced to wait for the appropriate kidney to be given. A non-matching kidney would be rejected by the patient's body.

Francia didn't have to think about it.

"I'll get tested," she said flatly. "Right away." I'll give you one of my kidneys if I can!"

Selena objected because it was such a large sacrifice, but Francia was adamant. Selena was like a sister to her. She couldn't face the thought of her pal in pain. It was conceivable to live a perfectly normal life with only one kidney.

The results were available within a few days. It was the outcome Francia had hoped for. She was a perfect match!

Before each operation, a potential organ donor must pass dozens of tests. Blood testing, diabetes tests, a CT scan, X-rays... Mental and emotional well-being must also be assessed. Normally, the process would take months. But Selena's health was rapidly deteriorating - it was an emergency. Francia completed all of the tests in one day. The date of the operation was set.

Francia returned home a few days later to find Selena had prepared a surprise for her. Her buddy presented her with a gift that was nicely wrapped in coloured paper and ribbons. Francia removed the paper to see a box shaped like a bible, a symbol of their shared faith. Their special friendship motto was engraved on the top: "A sister is a forever friend."

A kidney bean was found inside the packaging. Francia couldn't decide whether to laugh or cry since she was both happy and afraid.

Mandy and Francia remained in the hospital. Nurses arrived and left. Everyone smiled encouragingly, but they were ill with worry. Mandy fielded worried calls from the rest of the family: How did Selena fare? Why had there been no news?

The hours passed, and Selena's surgery was eventually completed. The surgeon walked in, grinning. It could only imply one thing. The procedure was a success!

Mandy could finally breathe again. She sat by Selena's bedside in a quiet room when she awoke from anaesthesia. Selena was unharmed! It was all that mattered in the world just now.

When Selena was able to move and speak, the nurses moved her bed next to Francia's. Selena extended her hand to squeeze her friend's hand.

"Thank you," she said quietly. "You've literally saved my life."

Their relief and gladness at seeing one other safe were incomparable.

The girls' recovery from the operation was difficult. The agony was terrible, and they developed sadness, which physicians warned them was usual following major surgery.

Both girls had scars and opted to flaunt them proudly. Selena didn't care what other people thought of her. Her body was alive and evolving. She understood that it would never be perfect, and she wanted to send a message to her followers that they, too, did not have to be perfect.

"Do you ever look back and regret what you've done?" Selena inquired of a buddy one day.

"Never!" Francia grinned. "I'll always be grateful that I was able to assist you."

Selena had faith in her. It felt great to know Francia was content with her decision.

Francia, too, had a question. "Does having a piece of my body inside you feel strange?"

"Very!" exclaimed Selena. It truly did!

Both girls had recovered and were full of energy after a few months. Francia had landed a role in a new program called Grown-ish. She couldn't wait to get back on set and do what she loved.

And what about Selena? Her next endeavour was the second season of 13 Reasons Why, on which she collaborated as an executive producer with her mother. She was ecstatic about the show they were collaborating on!

Selena's drive for reform was also garnering a lot of attention. As a spokesperson, she was making a difference, whether she was speaking at WE Day, endorsing UNICEF, performing benefit concerts, or just urging young people to be themselves, to reject hate, and to embrace compassion. TIME magazine featured her in a piece on female leaders in September. Ava DuVernay, Hillary Clinton, Ellen DeGeneres, and Gabby Douglas will appear alongside her. It was an honour to be in the presence of such wonderful women.

Then, on November 30, 2017, Selena received one of her career's highest honours: Billboard Woman of the Year. Many of pop's biggest names have won before: Beyoncé, Taylor Swift, Lady Gaga, Madonna, Katy Perry, Pink... Selena had previously earned the Billboard Chart-Topper award in 2015. However, Woman of the Year! This was incredible!

The award recognized success as a recording artist, contributions to the business, and leadership'. Selena was more aware than ever that she had a massive platform that night. It was a huge duty to be able to communicate with so many admirers all across the world. She wanted to put it to good use, to attempt to make the world a better place. And, of course, Selena knew just who she wanted to honour: Francia, her 'forever friend' who had saved her life. Selena, on the other hand, desired to accomplish more. Being a spokeswoman was great, but was there anything else she could do? Something that would truly benefit people on a daily basis? She'd had a glimpse of an idea in her head for a few months. It was now time to see if she could make it happen...

CHAPTER 22

A21

"All right, Selena, this is your key card. It provides access to both the main and side doors. The photocopier code is as follows. The first page of the handbook has your email address and extension number. If you have any IT problems, please contact the helpdesk at this number. "Do you have any questions?"

There was just too much to take in. It felt like the first day on the set of a new television show. Except that this time, the set was strangely... genuine. It was, after all, the first day of Selena's internship with A21, a non-profit anti-slavery organisation. She, like the other interns, would be working five days a week, performing a variety of chores while learning more about the organisation. Selena has never previously worked in an office. Her days were typically spent in recording studios, film sets, and concert halls. Everything was very new!

Except for... Selena smiled as she remembered the office scene in Taylor Swift's 'Bad Blood' video, where she assisted Taylor, as Catastrophe, in fighting a group of crooks before kicking her pal out the window. She made the decision to keep that thinking to herself!

Selena was a firm believer in A21's mission to end contemporary slavery worldwide. Human trafficking occurred on every continent. She was aware that it was taking place right here in California. People were being compelled to work for free in a variety of industries, ranging from farms and factories to restaurants and beauty salons. It was incredible that no one was talking about it. Why wasn't this front-page news every day?

"Just one question," Selena exclaimed happily. "What can I do first?"

'Reach. Rescue. Restore' was the A21 team's plan. First and foremost, they wished to avoid modern slavery by reaching out to vulnerable individuals. They also sought out and assisted people who were already enslaved. Finally, they gave care and support to former slaves, allowing them to live regular lives.

Selena's first assignment was to accompany a more experienced colleague to meet with liberated slaves. Their stories broke my heart. Listening to these men, women, and children, and delivering all the care and kindness she could, Selena realised she had made the right decision: this was the genuine, practical assistance she wanted to provide to those in need.

Selena had already felt like a member of the team by the end of the week. Her coworkers were very inspirational. They were extremely motivated. They were quite knowledgeable. Was it strange for them to have a pop star as a coworker, she wondered? They were way too professional to display it if it was. They simply treated her like any other intern. Finally, she could be a normal 25-year-old without the rest of the world watching!

But no one would let her get coffee.

"I thought interns all did that?" Selena burst out laughing. "You mean I've clocked all the nearest coffee shops for nothing?"

It was 1.30 a.m. on September 22nd. Selena was unable to sleep. She went about the house, made a drink, and ate a snack. She felt compelled to contact her fans as she browsed through her phone's alerts. She had taken a break from social media in recent months, but she had millions of admirers who loved and supported her, and she wanted them to know she loved them back.

She went live on Instagram. The video camera began filming with a single click. Selena Gomez was streaming live on the internet. What was it she wanted to say? She wasn't certain... but she'd find it out as she went!

"Hello, everybody!" Selena made a wave to the camera. "I'm doing a live video because I'm feeling like talking to you guys."

This felt great.

"I miss you!" she exclaimed. "I'm here, so... ask me anything." Let's give it a shot."

They succeeded. Fans from all across the world posed questions.

Was there going to be a new album? "Yes!"

Since Revival, Selena has not released an album. Along with A21 and her other projects, she was working on the next one. It has to be just right, something truly unique. She didn't want to rush anything.

Is this a new tour? "Yes!"

What about the press? Selena smirked.

In recent years, the media had caused her a great deal of stress and anxiety.

"Annoying!" That was the phrase. She then grinned. "But I've realised that anything I want to say can be said directly to you guys, right here." Selena enjoyed this new way of communicating!

There were numerous inquiries concerning social media. Selena thought it was ridiculous that everyone was enthralled with how many followers she had. "It's just a number," she said to her fans. "But I know it's the same for you guys." She understood how difficult it was for young people growing up with social media to be evaluated online. The pressure was the same whether you had 100 followers or 100 million.

The inquiries continued.

Was Selena content? "I am!" Life was good, and she wanted to share it with everyone! Some of the inquiries were serious in nature. Fans wanted to know how to deal with melancholy and panic attacks.

"Get to know yourself," Selena advised her followers. "Determine why you feel this way."

She had been through a lot of what her young followers were going through. Anxiety, followed by depression. Break-ups. Body shaming. Bullying. Living with a disease. It was a great feeling to be able to assist her admirers on their own journeys. And what about friendship? "My friends are the most amazing people in the whole world," Selena exclaimed, smiling. "My best friends have literally saved my life."

Next, a simple query... "Is that Taylor Swift?" She's fantastic! She's similar to my older sister. Everything I tell her."

Selena and her fans chatted for 40 minutes online. Speaking directly to her fans felt like chatting to a friend. It was great to be open, honest, and genuine. Her fans were always what kept her going. After all, it was they who permitted her to do what she loved. She was little concerned about how her management team and the media would respond in the morning. It didn't matter, though. The time was

2.10 a.m. Everyone else was fast asleep. It was only Selena and her admirers all over the world right now...

"I guess I'm going to wrap this up," she said to her followers. "But I'm going to do more of this."

Selena had one final thought.

"I appear insane. I'm suffering from a cold sore. And this zit. But I don't mind. This is my personality. Guys, good night. "I really like you."

CHAPTER 23

HAPPY BIRTHDAY, SELENA

Selena's birthday was on the 22nd of July. She was 26 years old.

Birthdays were always a time for Selena to reflect. So much had occurred in the previous year... Her placement at A21. Her kidney transplant saved her life. The honour of being awarded Billboard Woman of the Year. The end of her on-again, off-again relationship with Justin Bieber - Justin was now engaged. At the American Music Awards, she was named Favorite Pop/Rock Female Artist. 13 Reasons Why Becoming a Netflix Hit... A year of ups and downs? That was a massive understatement!

Friendship had kept Selena going through the spectacular highs and lows. Of course, she had Taylor and Francia, as well as her cousin Priscilla. Courtney, Ashley, Raquelle, Caroline, Connar, Sam, and Anna were also present. Selena was surrounded by individuals who genuinely cared for her. And her pals were determined to make her birthday weekend the best one yet! First up was a concert by Imagine Dragons, one of Selena's favourite bands. Grace VanderWaal, a young singer and ukulele player from Kansas who rose to popularity on America's Got Talent, opened the show. Simon Cowell was so taken with her that he dubbed her "the next Taylor Swift." Grace was a huge Selena fan, and the feeling was mutual.

When Selena arrived backstage to greet Grace, she said, "Happy birthday! Congratulations on your birthday! "Happy birthday, dear Selena, happy birthday!"

Grace led the song with her ukulele strumming. Flowers and cupcakes with Happy Birthday Selena inscribed in blue icing were on the table.

"A backstage party! Yay!" "This is sooooo sweet!" exclaimed Selena, hugging the young singer.

"When I heard you were coming, I knew I wanted to do something special," Grace explained.

Taylor was in New York, three thousand miles away, but she had also created a cake, homemade of course. She shared a photo of a giant sponge with pink frosting, a huge heart in the centre, and the words Gomez or Go Home. Selena burst out laughing. If only her pal had come to California. She missed her so much, and the cake made her drool just looking at it.

Then there's a pool party! Selena and her friends spent the day relaxing by the pool at her new Newport Beach home. Selena had just relocated from Los Angeles. She felt more at ease away from the stress of Los Angeles. Selena's image of heaven was Newport's miles of golden sandy beach, dramatic sunsets, and the blue water stretching to the horizon.

The biggest surprise, though, was yet to come...

"Where exactly are we going?" Selena inquired as her friends escorted her from the villa to the harbour.

Hundreds of gleaming white boats rocked on their moorings, while the setting sun was enveloped by a halo of fluffy pink clouds across the water. Selena took out her phone to take a picture. It was breathtaking.

"Almost there," Connar said. "Which one now?" "These boats are all the same!"

But then - there it was. Unmistakable! A sleek white cruiser decked out with banners and balloons. The skipper was waving from the deck. And what about inside the cabin? Selena burst out laughing. "You two! This is incredible!" Mandy, Brian, Selena's tiny half-sister Gracie, and her cousin Priscilla were all present. "Oh my god, I have never seen so much pasta!" she exclaimed. The girls had hired a chef to prepare Selena's favourite Italian foods, as well as some surprises for her. Ravioli, linguine, tortellini, fettuccine, and campanelle, to name a few. The aromas wafting from the small galley kitchen were amazing. It was going to be the most scrumptious party on the planet!

Waiters in tuxedos served the guests, and a string quartet played in the background while they ate. Then, as the golden sun faded away, fairy lights illuminated the cabin. It was a magical ending to a perfect day.

"It's been the best birthday," Selena remarked as she hugged her friends tightly. "Thank you!" says the author.

Selena's followers, known as Selenators, wanted to share the love on her big day as well: her birthday Instagram post received 10 million likes and 162,300 comments. It was just a number... but it felt fantastic to be connected to these incredible people all across the world.

It was time for Selena's family to return home, so they boarded the ship. It was well past Gracie's bedtime! Selena's friends dragged her onto the dancefloor as soon as she waved them off. Everyone had something corny they wanted to hear, and the DJ was taking requests!

Selena and her pals stayed up late talking and dancing. She was ecstatic to be surrounded by the people she cared about the most in the world. Will the coming year be another wild ride? Nobody has the ability to predict the future. Whatever happened, Selena felt she could handle anything with friends like them, her great family, and her devoted fans.

The contents of this book may not be copied, reproduced or transmitted without the express written permission of the author or publisher. Under no circumstances will the publisher or author be responsible or liable for any damages, compensation or monetary loss arising from the information contained in this book, whether directly or indirectly. .

Disclaimer Notice:

Although the author and publisher have made every effort to ensure the accuracy and completeness of the content, they do not, however, make any representations or warranties as to the accuracy, completeness, or reliability of the content. , suitability or availability of the information, products, services or related graphics contained in the book for any purpose. Readers are solely responsible for their use of the information contained in this book

Every effort has been made to make this book possible. If any omission or error has occurred unintentionally, the author and publisher will be happy to acknowledge it in upcoming versions.

Copyright © 2023

All rights reserved.

Printed in Great Britain
by Amazon